Devotionals for the Heart:

Revelations of God's Love

Edited by Alexis A. Goring

Devotionals for the Heart: Revelations of God's Love

All Scripture quotations are taken from the King James Version (KJV)

© 2020 by Alexis A. Goring

Cover Design by Teresa Tysinger (flower illustration by Freepik)

Senior Editor and Project Manager, Alexis A. Goring; Editor, Jessica Brodie; Proofreader, Sara L. Foust.

Published in the United States of America.

Dedication

To God be the glory for equipping my first team of devotional writers to create and share these encouraging words for Him!
Thank you for embarking on this devotional writing journey with me.

Contents

Acknowledgments

First and foremost, I want to thank God for orchestrating my Devotionals for the Heart series and putting this idea on my heart back in Fall 2017. My "God is Love" blog has grown as a ministry of encouragement because of this idea that blossomed.

Thank you, Jessica Brodie and Sara L. Foust, for being the most amazing editorial team! Your dedication, ongoing support, great ideas, professional expertise, and heart for sharing God's love with everyone on earth have made this book project possible.

Thank you to all my devotional writers whose words are published within this book! You are the first ones to join me on this "Devotionals for the Heart" book journey that began on my "God is Love" blog in January 2018. I want to thank you from the bottom of my heart for stepping out on faith and blessing my blog readers with your God-given words. I hope and pray each of you will continue to write for God. May your heart for sharing His love with the world reach people who need to hear the hope that is the Gospel of Jesus Christ.

Thank you to my parents and all my family members for believing in my dream to write, edit, and publish books! I appreciate your kind words, prayers, and steady support.

Thank you to my church family and pastors. You all are amazing! I appreciate each of you and I'm grateful for the role God has given each of us in the story of our lives.

Finally, thank you to all my readers from my blog to this book! Without you, my devotional writers and I would not know what it is like to let God use our words to encourage your hearts. We appreciate you and hope you will continue to be blessed by the words on the Devotionals for the Heart series and in this book.

Introduction

What started as a once-a-month devotional for my "God is Love" blog has bloomed into a triweekly ministry called "Devotionals for the Heart."

On July 27, 2015, Mary Manners contributed her first of many devotionals for my blog, blessing us for a season with her words. Then on January 3, 2017, I introduced readers to Laura Thomas, who took Mary's place and continued the tradition of writing monthly. When she was unable to continue contributing, God began leading me in a new direction.

It started simply: I wanted to find one Christian writer to replace Laura's monthly feature. I sent an email to American Christian Fiction Writers' extensive email list and was delighted to receive four responses within the first week. This inspired me to feature one devotional per week. But before I could implement that idea, more responses began flooding my inbox! It was time to discover how often people wanted to read devotionals.

Research revealed a desire for inspirational content at least three times a week. I also realized that this growing blog needed a graphic design and an original name. Through prayer, God placed "Devotionals for the Heart" in my soul. Next, my talented friend, Emilie Haney of EAH Creative, created a beautiful graphic design for the series, which continues to be used today!

At the end of each year, writers have a choice to continue to write for "Devotionals for the Heart." Though not everyone is able to stay, an increasing number of faithful writers remain part of the team. Meanwhile, the ministry keeps on growing. I am excited to see what God will do with these words of encouragement that He leads my writers to create as original "Devotionals for the Heart!"

Toward the end of 2018, God gave me the idea to turn this devotional blog series into a book. Most of my original writers agreed, and a few graciously offered to be part of the editorial team. This project took a bit longer than planned to be published, but I know that everything happens according to God's timing. Therefore, I believe this book became available for you right at the moment when God knew you would need it the most. I hope and pray it's a blessing to your heart. Thank you for reading!

Love,

Alexis A. Goring

Alexis A. Goring, MFA
Founder of "God is Love" blog
https://capturingtheidea.blogspot.com

Devotionals about Courage

www.capturingtheidea.blogspot.com

Answering God's Call

By Sara L. Foust

"But straightway Jesus spake unto them, saying, Be
of good cheer; it is I; be not afraid."
–Matthew 14:27 (KJV)

Has God ever asked You to do something scary?
Something intimidating? Something so far out of
your comfort zone you can't even see your bubble of
safety anymore?

He has asked me such a thing a few times now, and I
have been scared standing at the beginning of those
particular new jobs, often wondering "Why, Lord?
Why me? How does my willingness in this area of
life play into the bigger picture? What will I learn
through this experience?"

The truth is that we don't need to know the why,
how, or what. When God asks us to do something or
go somewhere, we should simply obey. Easier said
than done, right?

I very highly doubt the men and women in the Bible
wanted to walk into the middle of a wilderness with
no provisions whatsoever. Or that Peter wanted to
step out of the safety of that boat to tread atop the
water with Jesus. In fact, even the fleshly part of

Jesus, the part that felt the agony and the pain, didn't want to be crucified. But He prayed for strength and was willing to walk the line His Heavenly Father had laid out for him. I'm thankful I don't have to suffer like He did. To this point, every job God has given me has blessed me beyond measure and only added to the joy in my life.

Years ago, I was standing on the cusp of walking into the unknown. Just like the men and women of the Bible, God had asked me to do something for Him. I accepted the call and boarded a flight to travel all the way across the world. I left my babies, my husband, and my everyday, routine life to do something scary and intimidating far outside of my comfort zone.

But I was okay, because Jesus whispered in my heart that I should not be afraid. He said, "Be of good cheer, child. There's a reason you were called. There's a reason why you must go. There's a reason, a plan, a puzzle piece that needs to be placed by you."

I didn't know what those next two weeks, after my plane touched down on the other side of the world, held for me. But I did know I trusted God completely. Upon my return home, I had stories to share, photos to show off, and goodies I gave to my family. But more than that, I felt different in a bold and brave way because I obeyed God.

The experience made me who God needs me to be for the next step in my journey. I will not be afraid anymore to answer God's call and go where He sends me. Will you?

Let's pray: Thank You for blessing each of us with different talents and abilities, Lord. Use me, in my strengths and my weaknesses, in a way that glorifies You and shows others their need for You. Give me a job to do and give me the faith to do it without questioning why. Choose me, Lord, for Your next job! I want, more than anything, to be a blessing to others. In Jesus's name I pray. Amen.

Alexis A. Goring

Heroism Unleashed

By Gail Kittleson

"And after this Joseph of Arimathaea, being a disciple of Jesus, but secretly for fear of the Jews, besought Pilate that he might take away the body of Jesus: and Pilate gave him leave. He came therefore, and took the body of Jesus."
– John 19:38 (KJV)

Many heroes stand out in a crowd as muscular, brash, and egotistical. They can do superhuman feats, it seems.

The Olympics, though, highlight true heroes and heroines who enter their race with integrity and humility. Their tears when they win—or when they don't—testify they're in this for reasons of the heart.

A hero or heroine displays courage, bravery, or self-sacrifice for some greater good in the face of danger or adversity.

Joseph, a wealthy man who had a great deal to lose by choosing to support Jesus, qualifies as an unobtrusive hero. This member of the Jewish Council and a secret disciple of Jesus watched for the kingdom of God. He appears in all four Gospels, and his act of burying Jesus in the tomb he'd prepared for his own body garners our attention.

We read in John 19:38 that, in order to accomplish this feat, Joseph asked Pilate that he might take away the body of Jesus, and Pilate gave him permission. Nicodemus helped him, and we can imagine the two of them carrying their Lord to the tomb. They'd witnessed Jesus's wise dealings with the Pharisees and Sadducees, heard His teachings, and in spite of their fear of retribution from the powers that be, they believed.

The burial of Jesus catapults them into heroism. They had every reason to slink into the shadows with the rest of Jesus's disciples, every reason not to do what they did that night. The High Priest's henchmen were about, scanning for followers of Jesus.

But in a quiet, thoughtful way, Joseph and Nicodemus completed their work of love. A few women paid attention and risked their lives, too, revealing their devotion to the Savior.

Let's pray: Help us, Lord, in our everyday challenges, to display courage like Your servants Joseph and Nicodemus. In Jesus's Name I pray. Amen.

The Armor of God

By Sara L. Foust

"Put on the whole armor of God, that ye may be able
to stand against the wiles of the devil."
– Ephesians 6:11 (KJV)

Fall is my favorite time of year! I love the cooler
weather, the colors of fall leaves, the sounds of the
leaves touching gently to the earth, and most of all, I
enjoy our family's time outdoors. We plan camping
trips, day trips to Cades Cove, hikes, and picnics as
often as we can to soak in the beautiful East
Tennessee autumn.

But that's not the only reason I'm relieved to see
summer ending and fall beginning.

The summer of 2017 was not an easy one for me.
Usually, I look forward to the school break and
sleeping in late, but in 2017, those summer months
were some of the most stressful months I can
remember.

Once I went on the mission trip God called me to in
May 2017, I think I thought the devil would back off
and leave us alone for a while. Oh, how wrong I was!
He has ramped up his efforts, attacking every aspect
of our life. My children's behavior, my marriage, my

time, my rest, my body, my sanity, everything. I was deeply entrenched in one of the most intense battles of my life during that time, and I was exhausted!

Years ago, a dear friend of mine told me that each morning, before she gets out of bed, she prays to put on the full armor of God. It was such good advice, and I don't know why it has taken me so long to follow it. I had lots of excuses: I can't remember the Scripture or all the parts of the armor. I keep forgetting to type it up, and where would I put it that my kids wouldn't tear it down? I'm managing, so it's not a necessity … My excuses overflowed.

A couple of days ago, I finally put aside those excuses, typed out Ephesians 6:10-20, and hung it on my wall. When I wake up in the morning, I read the verses and pray each item of armor onto my spiritual body, especially focusing on the helmet of salvation to keep the enemy out of my mind and from affecting my thoughts (that's where he gets to me most easily). It is making such a huge difference in my daily walk!

Yes, life is still loud and crazy. No, I still can't say we have a precise schedule we follow. Yes, I'm still so tired I fall into bed at night and pass out. But I can feel a hedge of protection around my mind and heart, and around our home. I'm tired of being on the offense. I'm ready to fight back. And the armor of God, with the Word as my sword, is my weapon.

I encourage you to pray the armor of God onto your spiritual bodies each morning, too, and watch as God works in your life.

Let's pray: Not only did You leave Your Word (The Holy Bible) for me, Lord, but You also left armor for the battles of life, too! You left precise instructions about how to face the evils of this world and protect my mind, heart, and spirit. Thank You for loving me so completely, so wholly, so wonderfully. Help me find courage and boldness to serve You today and every day. In Jesus's name I pray. Amen.

Pulling Down Strongholds

By Nanci Rubin

"For the weapons of our warfare are not carnal, but mighty through God to the pulling down of strong holds; Casting down imaginations, and every high thing that exalteth itself against the knowledge of God, and bringing into captivity every thought to the obedience of Christ." – 2 Corinthians 10:4-5 (KJV)

The Christian is the enemy of Satan. The devil wants to defeat us by deception. He wants to keep us from the truth because he knows the truth will set us free.

I can't begin to tell you how many times the enemy has lied to me, and I bet he's lied to you, also. The common lies are: "You're no good." "You are not saved." "You're not going to make Heaven." "Your children are going to hell." "No one appreciates you." "Your husband doesn't love you anymore."

These thoughts bring fear. Thousands of lies are offered to your mind. When you accept them as your own, you begin to say with your mouth what the enemy has said to your mind. We have to bring every thought into the captivity of Christ. We must remember that life and death are in the power of the tongue (Proverbs 18:21).

When you audibly repeat the lies Satan gives you in thoughts, then you become fearful and live in torment. You are defeated before you even begin. Self-confidence is eroded, and an apathetic persona robs you of your energy. You feel trapped and unable to escape—a lie seeded in your mind.

Accept God's thoughts and promises, and repeat them out loud in faith. It brings peace to your heart. My dear mother used to take index cards, write Scripture on each one, and post them on her refrigerator. Every morning, she read them out loud. She placed God's Word in her mind, not what our enemy would like for us to confess.

Hold up your Bible and look at it. Contained therein are the thoughts of God. Live in the pages. Replace every thought the enemy gives you with one of God's thoughts. For every lie the enemy whispers, you must stand tall and counter it with the Word of God. When you do, he will have to flee. The Bible says in James 4:7 (KJV), "Submit yourselves therefore, to God. Resist the devil, and he will flee from you."

There is supernatural power in God's Word. I was put to the test several years ago when I stayed with my brother after his surgery. I knew in my spirit my brother was waging a war, and if I didn't stand in the gap right then, he would die. I prayed all night, walked the floor, and quoted every Scripture I knew over and over. I felt such power from God's Word. I knew in the spiritual realm my voice was heard. I was living John 7:38 (KJV), "He that believeth in me, as the Scripture hath said, out of his belly shall flow rivers of living water." I could feel living water rise within as I interceded for my brother.

Remember the battleground is in the mind, and the devil desires to infuse your thought life with his lies—lies to beat you down and give you fear and doubt. He has perfected his subtle ways through eons of time. You see, his primary approach is to attack our minds. He wants us to accept and act upon it.

God was very specific when he stated in Scripture for us to guard our hearts, being careful about what we see and hear and speak. We can't allow our senses to become garbage receptacles and dump just anything in there.

You can alter your condition and atmosphere by changing your thought life. Concentrate on God's great unchanging promises. You cannot sow seed-thoughts of sickness and live in an atmosphere of health. You have to see yourself as a conqueror before you have the victory. Take baby steps. Find the Scriptures that surround your area of need. Meditate on them and trust God.

Jesus Christ is the key to every issue we have in life. Life doesn't always turn out the way we want, but allowing our Savior access and seeking Him first will guarantee peaceful resolve.

Let's pray: Father God, I pray for my country, family, friends, and for You to repair what is broken and restore whatever is missing. Heal our hearts and our land. Give us the mind of Christ. In Jesus's name I pray. Amen.

Removing the "What If?"

By Melissa Henderson

"Fear thou not; for I am with thee: be not dismayed;
for I am thy God: I will strengthen thee; yea, I will
help thee; yea, I will uphold thee with the right hand
of my righteousness."
– Isaiah 41:10 (KJV)

Each year, at the scheduled time for my
mammogram, I become nervous. The reason for my
nervousness and fear is because thirteen years ago, I
went to the doctor for a routine mammogram and the
diagnosis was not what I expected. I was diagnosed
with breast cancer.

I am very good about getting my regular checkups
and mammograms. No changes had been noticed in
my body, and I was sure the same report would be
given that year. All would be fine, and an
appointment for the next year would be scheduled.
No problem.

Yet that particular visit was followed by a "call
back." The nurse on the phone told me there might be
something wrong with the film, so I needed to have
pictures taken again. No problem.

My husband drove me to have the additional pictures

done. We were so confident all was well, and he even sat in the car in the parking lot and waited for me.

After the second set of pictures was taken, I was asked to sit in a room and wait for the doctor. Another technician came in the room and told me she would view the results right there while I waited. We chatted and all was well—until her voice quieted and she said, "Mrs. Henderson, I will be right back. I need to get the doctor." No problem, or so I thought.

As the doctor entered the room, the atmosphere changed instantly. Fears of "what if?" ran through my mind. "What if there is a problem? What if I have cancer? What if I need surgery? Should someone go get my husband? My mother had breast cancer." These questions and more had my heart racing.

My first instinct was fear, when my first action should have been prayer. Yes, prayer came, but only after fear appeared first. Why didn't I remember to pray first? Praying always gives me comfort and peace. Yet that time, the "what ifs" got to me first.

The diagnosis of breast cancer, surgery, chemo-therapy, radiation, and medications I still have to take provided many lessons over these past thirteen years. Remember to pray. Read God's Word and soak in His message. Isaiah 41:10 tells us to not fear because He is our God. He will strengthen us and help us.

God strengthened me and my family. God helped us. God reminded us time and time again that He is always with us. We are blessed by His love.

I am praying this yearly mammogram will have a good report. No matter the outcome, I will lean on God and know that He is with me always.

Let's pray: Dear Lord, forgive me for the times when I worry. I know You have a plan for my life, and Your plan is always best. Forgive me for giving into worry instead of resting in Your comfort. Thank You for loving me. In Jesus's name I pray. Amen.

God is Always There

By Sara L. Foust

"For we walk by faith, not by sight."
– 2 Corinthians 5:7 (KJV)

When I wrote this devotional, my faith was thin. I was physically, emotionally, mentally, and spiritually exhausted. It had been that kind of year where I'd had wave after wave slam into me, and by the eleventh month, my snorkel was the only thing above water.

I am not the kind of person who has usually done a "word for the year" challenge. But that particular year, without even really thinking about it, the word "courage" came to me very early on. I knew I would need immense amounts of courage to go on my mission trip. I thought that would be the biggest obstacle that I would face. I was wrong.

My son was diagnosed with autism.

My daughter began mental health therapy.

My marriage came to the beginning of the end.

My TMJ condition needed joint surgery with a disc removal and skin graft.

My church wasn't my church anymore.

But through it all, I learned one very important lesson: God loves me, no matter what decisions I make and no matter what mental state I am in. He loves me unconditionally, unendingly, and without blame. His love pours out from His heart to mine like pure spring water—clear, unaltered, unhindered love.

God's unconditional love was the only saving grace I had during those hard times. It was the only beacon of light when things looked dark. God's undying love for us is real, honest, time-tested, and true.

So rather than the above list in the "cons" column, here's what I'm choosing to focus on:

My son spoke to his Pre-K teacher for the first time and he learned a ton of new words that he still uses freely at home.

My daughter now sleeps through the night, most of the time in her own room. She is confident, happy, and growing.

My marriage produced three beautiful biological and two wonderful adopted children, and I learned immense amounts about myself.

I survived the surgery for my TMJ condition.

My church family, though I am not able to be present with them, still loves me, and God will lead me to another church home.

Ultimately, I've realized God is never going to leave me, and He is never going to leave you. He wants us to cry out to Him in the middle of that black ocean called worry, fear, dread, sickness, divorce, or temptation. Whatever your ocean is called, He is there.

He is always there.

Let's pray: There are times, Lord, when I'm not sure I'll ever reach the light at the end of the tunnel. But You know what is best for me. You know why I go through each storm. I will continue to trust in You and praise You in the middle of my struggles. You are good to me, and I love You. Thank You for loving me. Give me strength to stand up and fight until I reach the other side. In Jesus's name I pray. Amen.

Alexis A. Goring

Devotionals about Discipline

www.capturingtheidea.blogspot.com

A Year with God

By Sara L. Foust

"For I am persuaded, that neither death, nor life, nor angels, nor principalities, nor powers, nor things present, nor things to come, Nor height, nor depth, nor any other creature, shall be able to separate us from the love of God, which is in Christ Jesus our Lord." – Romans 8:38-39 (KJV)

Whenever we celebrate the turn of a new year, we set our resolutions high, such as believing that we can lose twenty-five pounds by summertime.

Maybe your goals don't refer to weight loss but, rather, to success in your career. I know I have penned a few writing-career-related goals myself. Maybe your goals refer to your family life, your marriage, travel, or how many books you'd like to read this year. But do you have any goals that relate to your spiritual relationship with God?

I have to admit, my first draft didn't, and that won't do at all. Once I realized what my list was missing, I dropped everything down and opened goal number one up for this: I want to spend quality time with God every morning, studying The Holy Bible and in quiet meditation with Him.

Around here, that is a tall order, because I have five children. It is never, I mean never, quiet around here. And when it is, I'd better see where everyone is because someone is doing something they shouldn't be doing.

But I realized toward the close of 2017 that even though I was still reading my Bible during my morning study times, I wasn't really digesting the words and internalizing them in order to grow in my faith. That had to change.

So for 2018, I made a goal of going to a room—even if it has to be the bathroom—by myself and reading The Bible. I want my children to see me studying God's Word, but I also know that I need that morning one-on-one time with my Savior so I can make it through the day.

We don't know what will come this year. No doubt we will experience loss to some degree. We will experience joy, success, and satisfaction to some degree. We will have trials that feel like vertical mountains we must scale. We will have victory, standing on the top of those "impassable" trials and looking back on them with pride that God helped us through each step.

Romans 8:38-39 reminds us that no matter where we go, what we face, or how low (or high) we get, God is there. He will be with you and me in each and every moment, with each breath and each blink of our eyes, because He loves us. Unconditionally. Unequivocally. Eternally. Perfectly.

Let's make the decision right now to spend the year being aware of His presence in our lives, dedicated to growing in our faith, and continuously striving to work for Him.

Let's pray: Lord, please come into my daily study time with You. Open my eyes to the truths of Your Word, and allow me time each and every day to read my Bible, understand, and meditate with You. If there are new things I need to learn, help me see them. If there are old things I need to learn again in a new way, please show me. In Jesus's name I pray. Amen.

Devotionals about Tough Love and Hardship

www.capturingtheidea.blogspot.com

God's Workmanship

By Sara L. Foust

"For we are His workmanship, created in Christ Jesus
unto good works, which God hath before ordained
that we should walk in them."
– Ephesians 2:10 (KJV)

The above Bible verse has been on my heart a lot
lately. First, when I returned from my mission trip in
May. Then it spurred the idea for my recent blog post
on my website. And today, again, as I write this
newest thought, I can't get this verse out of my mind.

As my friend Becky and I drove to a weekend event
at the Grainger County Tomato Festival recently, the
topic of our health came up, as it does often. I have
struggled with depression since I was a young girl,
and many times in my life I have wondered why in
the world I had to suffer with such a complicated,
unseen, stigmatized disease. Years ago, my cousin
pointed out to me that I shouldn't feel embarrassed or
badly about my disease. It isn't necessarily
something I can completely control.

After all, someone with diabetes, heart disease, or
arthritis is rarely chastised for having a disease. It
isn't something they can help, right? I am thankful
for this reminder and especially thankful for the

journey of self-discovery and self-acceptance it created.

Since that conversation, God has shown me just how carefully He crafted me. I am precious, handcrafted, unique, and made with care. God didn't randomly grab a bunch of ingredients and throw them into my DNA pot. No! He handpicked each ingredient with intention, including whatever element it is in my brain that makes me susceptible to depression. I may not understand why I have it. My cousin may not understand why she has rheumatoid arthritis. My friend may not understand why she has dysautonomia. But I firmly believe, without a shadow of a doubt, there is a reason.

Let's say that again: There is a reason. Knowing the Bible tells us "all things work together for good to them that love God" (Romans 8:28, KJV), it must be a good reason—for our good and the good of others. Since I accepted that part of me and began telling my story, God has given me opportunities to encourage others who have similar problems.

Unless I possess firsthand knowledge of a disease or situation, while I may feel empathetic, it is hard to fully and completely understand how a person feels. Not the way the person experiencing it does, anyway. Because I know what it's like in the darkness of depression and the joy of finding light, I can help others who are struggling to find God's light, His peace and the wonder of God's love.

It may sound strange to some, but I am thankful for my disease. It makes me a more humble, understanding, and compassionate person. It draws me closer to God, for in the "down" times I must draw close to Him to keep my head above water. And it allows me to understand a niche of people whom I could potentially be blessed to help.

It's often hard to embrace a diagnosis as a good thing, but I am trying to keep it in a positive perspective and keep my focus on the good that can come from a disease in the form of helping another. I'm also trying hard to be thankful for a loving God who created me just as I am. It is a blessing to be made with care and to know I am God's workmanship.

Let's pray: Lord, thank You for all the parts of me. Thank You for creating me with intention and knowing exactly which pieces to put in me. I ask that You will allow me to be a blessing to someone today and every day. Help me to help someone else. In Jesus's name I pray. Amen.

What is Your Idol?

By Nanci Rubin

"Son of man, these men have set up their idols in
their heart, and put the stumbling block of their
iniquity before their face: should I be enquired of at
all by them? Therefore speak unto them, and say unto
them, Thus saith the Lord God; Every man of the
house of Israel that setteth up his idols in his heart,
and putteth the stumbling block of his iniquity before
his face, and cometh to the prophet; I the Lord will
answer him that cometh according to the multitude of
his idols."
– Ezekiel 14:3-4 (KJV)

God has made a way of escape for every situation we
might find ourselves in. He doesn't want us in
bondage. We're so quick to step into a trap because
the idol seems harmless. I've fallen into traps
throughout my Christian walk and was stunned by
how innocent it all seemed.

Here's an example of my own idol-making
experience: When I was in the workforce, I was the
classic workaholic. I loved my job. I worked
overtime and gave no thought to my husband when
he came home from his job to an empty house and
less-than-desirable meals. I allowed the job to
encroach into my prayer life, and soon I became too

tired to go to church midweek. Finally Sundays were out because I had household duties and shopping to do on Saturday, so Sunday became my own personal day of rest. I was blinded to the danger of the idol I was setting up in my life.

Then God began to intervene in a way I never suspected.

God sent another nurse into the practice who sabotaged me and caused me so much grief. She actually told me she was going to get my job, and she did. God not only allowed this, but He also orchestrated it—all to get me away from the idol I was making in my life. He cares enough to steer us back when we get off track.

Take an internal check. Is there anything in your life that detracts or interferes with your serving God? He desires our first fruits, not just of your increase, but your time. We are admonished to not have any gods before Him. That was His first commandment, for the Bible says in Exodus 20:3 (KJV), "Thou shalt have no other gods before me."

Since God made this His first commandment, it's important to Him, but more so for us. My writing, at times, pulls me back into my old work habits. I love writing, and one would ask, "How could that be wrong?"

The writing isn't! It's the order I've placed it in. Since I am being called to correction, I will do so post haste. I want nothing to come between my Heavenly Father and myself. Nothing else matters. Maintaining a balanced Christian life is difficult, and you can't do it alone. Only God can keep you on an even keel.

Let's pray: Father God, create in me the heart of a servant that I might not sin against You. When I'm in error, be quick to correct my steps. Thank You for Your constant care of us, Your children. In Jesus's name I pray. Amen.

The Last Laugh

By Quantrilla Ard

"And Abram said, 'Lord God, what wilt thou give
me, seeing I go childless, and the steward of my
house is this Eliezer of Damascus?'"
– Genesis 15:2 (KJV)

One of my dear children loves to get the last laugh
when things happen in our family.

The words "That's what you get, baby!" rang out
loud and clear one day, to my surprise, as my two-
year-old chided her brothers for something they had
done. She is undoubtedly spirited and full of passion
when identifying her brothers' mishaps. Of course,
she has a few challenges identifying her own. This,
coupled with her comedic and ironic timing, makes
laughter an everyday occurrence. With so many
opportunities for giggles, I am reminded of the old
adage, "He who laughs last, laughs best."

I'm so glad God has a sense of humor. Abraham and
Sarah would probably agree.

Abraham and Sarah had waited, albeit not so
patiently, for God to keep His promise to them by
giving them a son with whom He would establish His
covenant. Sarah was long past childbearing age and

well into her sunset years. Abraham was knocking on one hundred. God's timing was then and is now often vastly different from our own.

In their story, the first laugh comes from Abraham, in his ninety-ninth year as God changes his name and again calls him to remember the promise He made years earlier, as the story details in Genesis 17:17. The second laugh comes from Sarah after a visit from three men, one of whom just happens to be God Himself (Genesis 18:12). They were hopeful yet equally despondent from the trials of waiting. One son, Ishmael, through Sarah's servant Hagar, had to be sent away because Sarah's desperation and subsequent insecurity had gotten the best of her. They were spent.

One question changes everything: "Is anything too hard for the Lord?" God asks as He calls Sarah out for laughing. And I can imagine in my mind's eye that God is laughing to Himself at the look on her face. Within the year, as God had promised and re-promised, Isaac was born. And guess what Isaac's name means? Yep, you guessed it: "He laughs."

Is there a place in your life that seems desolate and barren? A place that feels forgotten? Have you held out hope only to see another year pass without God fulfilling a promise in or to you? I know I have. I have laughed at reminders that God sent my way, thinking my season has expired and it's just too much to expect that things will turn out the way He said they would. And then I hear God ask me, thousands of years later, just as He asked Sarah, "Is there anything too hard for the Lord?"

The answer is a resounding no. I see His promises come to pass in His timing, not my own. I wait sometimes patiently, sometimes not, thankful He loves me anyway. I can rejoice in my "Isaac" circumstances, and see that God indeed gets the last laugh.

Nothing is too hard for the Lord. Absolutely nothing.

Let's pray: Lord, Your timing is perfect. My patience still needs a little work. Thank You for knowing what's best and calming my anxious heart while I wait. Help me to remember Your delay is not Your denial, and that any time spent waiting will always be worth it. May You get the glory in the wait. In Jesus's name I pray. Amen.

Devotionals about Prayer and Hardship

www.capturingtheidea.blogspot.com

Unspoken Prayers

By Melissa Henderson

"Likewise the Spirit also helpeth our infirmities: for we know not what we should pray for as we ought: but the Spirit itself maketh intercession for us with groanings which cannot be uttered."
– Romans 8:26 (KJV)

The words wouldn't come. My heart was heavy. My body was exhausted from worry for a family member who had been making terrible life decisions. I had taken matters into my own hands, thinking I could fix everything. I had not prayed to ask for help. Why did I not go to God first?

Praying doesn't mean everything will turn out the way I want things to be. Praying gives me a relationship with God. He knows my thoughts before I think or speak.

Yet years ago, I held on to my thinking of how life would be different for my family member if only I could help. I offered to go along on doctor visits, to cook special meals, to take the person on outings every week, and much more.

If only these offers would make the person happy and find a way out of the dangerous decisions they were making. If only I could fix this problem and make them feel better. I truly wanted to help.

Worry and anxiety consumed my days and nights. Just thinking about the wrong decisions the person was making made me physically ill. Knowing the potential of this wonderful family member brought tears more than once or twice. Watching them take a downward spiral broke my heart.

Why won't they listen? Why do they repeat bad behavior over and over, not only hurting themselves but hurting the people around them? Why? Questions came over and over.

Yet I had not gone to God during those moments.

In fact, I may have complained and shown a less-than-friendly attitude when talking with God about the situation. I'll admit that. My questions continued to be, "Why is this happening? Why are You letting this happen?" Why?

Instead of surrendering to God and placing the burden at His feet, I tried to carry the burden alone. After a period of time passed, my body was weak from stress, worry, and sadness. Finally, I surrendered the situation to the Father.

On my knees, I asked for His forgiveness for not coming to Him sooner. I thanked Him for the love that He provides freely each and every moment. I didn't have special words. I spoke from my heart. I did not have a beautiful, thought-out prayer. My prayer began with groans and sighs that were too deep for words.

God found me in my despair, and He lifted me up. As I gave the situation to Him, my burden lightened and peace was found.

Shortly after that surrender, life began to change in a wonderful way for my family member. I know God was listening, and He answered prayers in His way and in His time.

God reminded me to take my burdens to Him and to trust that He will handle the outcome.

Let's pray: Father God, in times of need, I cry out to You. Thank You for answering me in Your timing and in Your way. I am impatient at times. Please forgive me for my need to fix things immediately. Your timing is always best. I may never know the answers to some questions, and that is okay. I trust You. In Jesus's name I pray. Amen.

The Storms of Life

By Paula Moldenhauer

"Then they cry unto the Lord in their trouble, and he
bringeth them out of their distresses. He maketh the
storm a calm, so that the waves thereof are still. Then
are they glad because they be quiet; so he bringeth
them unto their desired haven. Oh that men would
praise the Lord for his goodness, and for his
wonderful works to the children of men!"
– Psalm 107:28-31 (KJV)

Sometimes storms come with angry fury. Wind-
whipped tree branches are forced to the ground,
majestic boughs bending; beautiful leaves are
shredded and flung into the sky. Hail pelts, bruising
flowers and crushing tender plants. Living, breathing
creatures cower wherever shelter is found.
Trembling, they seek safety.

Other storm systems are more quiet, but no less
incessant. Snow falls for hours; hours stretch to days.
Gray-white clouds hide the sun and the stars. The
storm is relentless, but silent, ever falling, covering
the world beneath, burying any sign of life.
Sometimes its weight presses upon barren limbs,
piling upon them until the strong trees crack
underneath the cold, white mounds. And the living
huddle anywhere warmth can be found. They eye

their reserves, hoping they have enough to outlast the ever falling, quietly swirling powder.

The storms in our life have different names: illness, relationships, finances, grief, wounds, overwhelming busyness ... the list goes on. Sometimes they attack with a fury that leaves us trembling and breathless. Other times they linger indefinitely, demanding fortitude and perseverance beyond our comprehension.

But always storms make us cry for a safe place.

The Bible tells about a time Paul, traveling by ship, faced a wind of typhoon strength. Acts 27:20 (KJV) tells us, "And when neither sun nor stars in many days appeared, and no small tempest lay on us, all hope that we should be saved was then taken away."

The storm was frightening, and it was long. The sailors gave up on their lives. But God sent an angel to Paul to tell him not to be afraid—that God's plans for him required his life be spared.

Paul also faced a long, silent storm. He called it his thorn in the flesh and asked three times that God take it away. But God didn't. According to 2 Corinthians 12:9a (KJV), He simply told Paul, "...My grace is sufficient for thee: for my strength is made perfect in weakness."

These stories remind me of something I heard from Max Lucado. He said everything that comes our way is first sifted through the Lord's hands, and that we should submit to God's Lordship in our life, even in the storms.

At one level I understand this—even feel protected by it. But when something really hurts, I feel I've gotten the raw end of the deal.

Why does He allow such pain?

In the long run, I always come back to the same truth. Though I don't understand why bad stuff happens, I don't want to walk through a gale force wind without my Father God. I can question His love and His wisdom or embrace the truth: God is love. God is wisdom.

God has our eternal good in mind at all times. His love is ever-present, always available, and abounding to us. He is there when we cry out to Him.

Sometimes God rescues us from the storm. I'm comforted by Psalm 107:28-30 (KJV) that says, "Then they cry unto the Lord in their trouble, and he bringeth them out of their distresses. He maketh the storm a calm, so that the waves thereof are still. Then are they glad because they be quiet; so he bringeth them unto their desired haven."

Other times the storm continues, unabated, and He whispers, as He did to Paul in 2 Corinthians 12:9a (KJV). He says, "My grace is sufficient for thee: for my strength is made perfect in weakness." No matter how hard a storm rages or how long it lasts, our safe place is always the same: in God's arms. Snuggled there, our heart is at rest.

Let's pray: Dear God, when it fits Your perfect plan, I ask that You still the storm. When in Your wisdom You allow a storm, focus my mind and emotions on Your sufficient grace. Give me new understanding to see and respond to my situation from Your perspective. Empower me to rest in Your arms and to live in Your peace that passes all understanding. In Jesus's name I pray. Amen.

Finding Joy

By Sara L. Foust

"And we know that all things work together for good to them that love God, to them who are the called according to His purpose." – Romans 8:28 (KJV)

Romans 8:28 is one of my favorite Bible verses. I love its promise that God is working for my good at all times. It has been comforting to me in times of grief, stress, and fear. It has been a reminder when I'm struggling about whether or not God's plan is good for me.

I was saved when I was nineteen and began attending church on a regular basis. All of a sudden, as a new Christian and as a young adult who was still trying to figure out this life, I was exposed to preaching and teaching like I'd never heard before, with a set of unspoken church "rules" that I had to absorb unconsciously. There was a new abundance of information to take in and process.

However, I misunderstood one of these new rules. One day, I woke with the realization that I believed God didn't care if I was happy or not. Wow—how did I come to believe this?

Through no fault of anyone but myself, I'd taken

Scripture and preaching out of context.

I'd taken the lesson that we should learn to be content in all situations (Philippians 4:11-13) to mean that no matter how unhappy we are, we shouldn't allow ourselves to be unhappy. I thought that we should always put on a brave face and learn to smile through the midst of every struggle and that every bad thing in our lives is part of God's plan, just like the good things.

But that doesn't make complete sense. We have free will (Galatians 5:13), and that means we have the ability to make wrong decisions, ones that affect the people around us, too. If everyone were to follow God's leading for every decision, every single moment of every single day, then I could rest assured that everything that happened to me was, in fact, for my good. But as imperfect, sinful human beings, this isn't possible. Things happen, and people make bad decisions. Does that mean God wanted those decisions to negatively affect me? No, I don't believe so.

Rather, what I think God wants me to see is that He is always there for me during the struggles. His plan is for my good, and when things don't go according to His plan, He hurts right along with me. And the knowledge that He is with me, on my side and on your side, is where we can find the joy amid the pain.

Now, don't get me wrong. God doesn't want us to sin in order to find "happiness." Our true happiness lies in following His will for us, in doing our best to follow His path, despite what is going on around us. But God does want us to have a fulfilled, enjoyable life (John 10:10), not one filled with misery where we pretend everything is okay because we are supposed to. No! He wants joy for us. He does care if we find it.

I've come to see that when a negative, sin-filled situation or decision someone else has made is affecting me negatively, it is okay to remove myself from that situation. It is okay to separate myself in order to try to relocate God's path, then pray for the person or situation from a distance in order to protect my spiritual morality.

Whether it be a best friend, a family member, or a church, if we have the sense that the trend is leading us away from God's will for our lives, then it is our duty to resist and go our way—the way God is planning, with good roads in our future (Proverbs 3:5-6).

Let's pray: Dear God, You are a compassionate, caring Father, and I know You want me to thrive and find joy. Life in this world is often hard. Sometimes its challenges come from the people around me. I ask You to give me discernment about what is right and wrong and courage to follow Your leading in all situations. Help me walk the straight and narrow way that You have planned for me and not get distracted and sidetracked. In Jesus's name I pray. Amen.

Rejoicing in the Lord Always

By Melissa Henderson

"Rejoice in the Lord always: and again I say,
Rejoice."
– Philippians 4:4 (KJV)

Rejoicing during difficult times can often be stressful. How can we rejoice when bills are overdue, our health is in jeopardy, the news is filled with scary information, and we are not sure what will happen next?

God gives us a spirit of power and love and of sound mind. Anxiety and fear do not come from the Lord. So what do we do when troubled times enter our lives?

We pray. We talk with God, sharing our hopes and fears with Him. He already knows what we are thinking. He wants us to come to Him. He is waiting with open arms.

Recently, my husband and I moved from Virginia to South Carolina. We prayed and asked God to give us the wisdom, discernment, and revelation as to what He wanted us to do about the move.

We had our times of uncertainty and fear. Yet each

time we paused and prayed, God gave us a feeling of calm and comfort.

Remembering to praise Him and rejoice in Him each and every day made our move easier. Even with road bumps along the way, we know God is with us, and we will rejoice again and again. He is in charge, and He has a plan for our lives.

Have you thanked God for His blessings? Have you rejoiced in His love and mercies today? Share time with God, and you will be refreshed as you rejoice.

Let's pray: Father God, when I rise in the morning and when I rest my head at night, let me recall Your mercies and love. I pray that I will rejoice in Your love and feel the calm and peace that only You can provide. In Jesus's name I pray. Amen.

Restoring Your Soul

By Melissa Henderson

"He restoreth my soul: he leadeth me in the paths of
righteousness for his name's sake."
– Psalm 23:3 (KJV)

Every moment of each day has the potential to be
filled with hope or filled with despair.

Daily living may include activities that give us joy or
bring on stress—smiles one moment and tears the
next, from employment worries, financial concerns,
health issues, relationship challenges, and to-do lists
invading our thoughts and making our hearts beat
faster and our pulse feel like we're running a never-
ending race. We can become consumed with worry.

Have you ever experienced one of those days? A day
when everything seemed to be going wrong? A time
when the car wouldn't start, the bills were overdue,
the dinner burned on the stove, the laundry machine
overflowed onto the floor, the school called with
news of a bad situation or any other worrisome
event?

Pause for a moment. In those seemingly endless
situations where you felt like all you could do was
fall to the floor and cry, what was your initial

reaction? What was your response to everything happening around you? What about things you have no control over? What about things you do have control over, and they still went the wrong way?

Did you blame someone? Did you blame God? What were the first words out of your mouth or the first thoughts in your mind? Was your question something like, "Why God? Why do bad things keep happening to my family and me? What is the reason? How can we go on like this? I can't take this anymore. I don't know what to do."

I have experienced those awful days—times when my heart has broken into pieces and I felt deeply at a loss for a remedy to the situation. Through a medical diagnosis of breast cancer and the after-effects of surgery and treatment, to the loss of both of my parents, to job changes and financial concerns and so much more, I have been that person who fell to my knees and asked, "Why? Lord, are You trying to teach me something? What is the purpose in all this mess?"

The storms of life hit, and thankfully, I have a way to find peace and comfort. Yes, I still encounter the storms and stumble through them. But I am not alone. You are not alone.

Through learning to rely on God and not myself, I found an answer to help me. No, the problems aren't all "fixed." Yet there is one response to my worry that comforts me the most.

You may ask, "What? How can anyone find comfort in the saddest of times?"

My answer is this: Call out to God. Cry to Him. Give Him your joys and your concerns. He knows your heart already. He is waiting for you. Share your thoughts and your pain with Him. Talk with God. He is ready to restore your soul.

Saying His name provides comfort for me. Father. Jesus. God. Savior. Creator. Those are just some of His names. Breathe in and say His name. Breathe out and say His name. Concentrate on Him.

Pause and say His name. Call to Him. He is listening. Let Him restore your soul.

Problems and stressful times will come and go. God will always be here for us. Remember that His love is overflowing and never-ending. He loves you.

Let's pray: Thank You, Father God, for renewing me each and every day. You restore my soul and give me peace and comfort. You are my redeemer and sustainer. Please continue to restore my soul. In Jesus's name I pray. Amen.

God's Word in All Seasons

By Sara L. Foust

"All Scripture is given by inspiration of God, and is profitable for doctrine, for reproof, for correction, for instruction in righteousness."
– 2 Timothy 3:16 (KJV)

There are times in my life when I don't know exactly what to do, such as how to react to an event or comment or how to deal with the heaviness of grief. I am so thankful that God loved us enough to leave a guidebook for us in His Word, The Holy Bible.

His Word is perfect, entire, and useful in every situation. No matter what I face, I can turn to the Bible and find an answer. Sometimes the same exact verses that gave me answers in grief are the ones that can give me direction in joy. I love how I can read God's Word on a daily basis and learn something new every time.

Several years ago, I realized spending time in quiet meditation studying the Bible was an important act of faith. I began taking some time each morning to read, pray, and sit quietly in His presence. As the number of children increased in my home, the quiet part has become much more difficult. But I find that if I forget or push aside my one-on-one time with His Word, my days are tougher.

God's Word can be all things to all people. It is perfect for teaching, admonishing, preaching, ministering, witnessing, encouraging, strengthening, and comforting. He left the Word with a purpose, with a great love for His children, so that we can find each of those things no matter what challenges, blessings, or fears lay ahead of us.

I've included some of my favorite verses below. These are ones I have especially turned to in times when I needed His comfort and direction, and I've found that, even though my situation changes, I can find exactly what I need in these verses every time.

This one is especially good for times of grief or when I am hurting: "He healeth the broken in heart, and bindeth up their wounds. He telleth the number of the stars; He calleth them all by their names. Great is our Lord, and of great power: His understanding is infinite." – Psalm 147:3-5 (KJV)

This one is wonderful for times when I feel confused and need direction: "God hath not given us the spirit of fear; but of power, and of love, and of a sound mind." – 2 Timothy 1:7 (KJV)

This one is good for times when I am questioning why: "And we know that all things work together for good to them that love God, to them who are the called according to His purpose." – Romans 8:28 (KJV)

This one is good when I am overly stressed and need to be reminded that I am God's child and, therefore, I can find refreshment in Him: "And be not conformed to this world: but be ye transformed by the renewing of your mind, that ye may prove what is that good, and acceptable, and perfect, will of God." – Romans 12:2 (KJV)

This one is perfect for times when I need to be reminded that prayer works, just not always on my time: "And if we know that He hear us, whatsoever we ask, we know that we have the petitions that we desired of Him." – 1 John 5:15 (KJV)

And finally, this one is good when I need to be reminded of my purpose here: "But whoso looketh into the perfect law of liberty, and continueth therein, he being not a forgetful hearer, but a doer of the work, this man shall be blessed in his deed." – James 1:25 (KJV)

I hope that you are encouraged to study God's Word and glean your own favorite verses for the different seasons of your life.

Let's pray: Dear God, without Your Word, Your Guidebook, Your Wisdom written down in terms I can understand, I would be so lost. Thank You for knowing I would need instruction and being willing to give me perfect words that fit everything I face. Help me remember to turn to Your Word, Lord, when I need instruction, clarity, and encouragement. Help me to be open to what You show me through Your Word. In Jesus's name I pray. Amen.

He Left Us Everything

By Nanci Rubin

"And for this cause He, (Jesus) is the mediator of the new testament, that by means of death, for the redemption of the transgressors that were under the first testament, they which are called might receive the promise of eternal inheritance."
– Hebrews 9:15 (KJV)

I'm reading a memoir by Plum Johnson, *They Left Us Everything.* It is written by a woman who recently lost her mother, her father had died years previously, and she's in the process of cleaning out the family home. A house she and her three brothers called home for more than half a century. She, now in middle age, along with her brothers, is left to empty out a house of twenty-three rooms. Every corner in every room offers a memory. Middle-agers who have gone through caregiving and burying our mothers will find this book relatable.

This book has opened a plethora of memories for me. I lost my mom two years ago, and I still find pieces of memories in out-of-the-way places, little things that remind me of how much I miss her.

This morning I got up early, not because I wanted to,

but because my darling cat, Juliette, was hungry. She has learned to wake me gently, and I appreciate her respecting my rest. As I got up to feed her, I caught a glimpse of the book, and the title grabbed me in a profound way: *They Left Us Everything.* I saw Jesus in this title! I realized that through Him, God has left us everything.

I was reminded of a time twenty years ago, shortly after my brother died. Losing him at such a young age rocked my world. I'd thought we'd grow old together. It was a difficult time for me, and grief devastated me. It was during my caterwauling and pity party that God spoke to my spirit, reminding me that He understood my grief. He'd sacrificed His Son for humanity. It quickly put things in perspective.

I bemoaned why Ronnie, my brother, wasn't healed and the unfairness of it all. God is so patient with us. We can't know everything. It was Ronnie's time. He'd rededicated his life to Christ before passing, and he was actually ready. I wasn't. I didn't want him to leave. But God reminded me that the blood of Jesus, the cross, and the Comforter are all we need in this life to overcome the world and our eternal enemy. He's done all He's going to do. The rest is up to us.

I began to search the Scriptures to confirm what God shared with me.

John 3:16 (KJV), the very first Scripture I committed

to memory, took on a whole new meaning. It reads, "For God so loved the world, that He gave His only begotten Son, that whosoever believeth in Him should not perish, but have everlasting life."

The second Scripture that came to me was John 14:16-18 (KJV), "And I will pray the Father, and He shall give you another comforter, that He may abide with you forever; even the Spirit of truth, whom the world cannot receive, because it seeth Him not, neither knoweth Him, but ye know Him, for He dwelleth in you and shall be in you. I will not leave you comfortless, I will come to you."

The third Scripture is found in Ephesians 1:7 (KJV), which reads, "In whom we have redemption through His blood, the forgiveness of sins, according to the riches of His grace."

The fourth Scripture was Revelation 12:11 (KJV), "And they overcame Him by the blood of the Lamb, and by the word of their testimony, and they loved not their lives unto the death."

Before I knew Jesus Christ as my Savior, these Scriptures were just words. They didn't gird me, heal me, or penetrate the armor I wore daily to circumvent any emotional conflict. I didn't want to feel anything. Many of us walk around numb, defeated, and allowing the cares of this life to drag us down.

After I accepted Jesus Christ as my Savior, I began to understand the weapons of our spiritual warfare, the power in the blood of Jesus Christ and the guidance from the Holy Spirit. Finally, I knew what God the Father meant by those verses in His Word, The Holy Bible. Accepting Jesus opened my blind eyes to see and my deaf ears to hear. I saw the world around me with the blinders taken off. He really did leave us *everything*.

What's even better? The best is yet to come!

Let's pray: Father God, thank You for Your promise to us, Your children, of eternal life with You when we accept Your Son, Jesus Christ. Our inheritance is rich in You and in Your Son who is our Savior. In Jesus's name I pray. Amen.

Alexis A. Goring

Devotionals about Peace and Trust

Devotionals for the Heart

www.capturingtheidea.blogspot.com

Choosing the Light

By Gail Kittleson

"Through the tender mercy of our God; whereby the
dayspring from on high hath visited us, To give light
to them that sit in darkness and in the shadow of
death, to guide our feet into the way of peace."
– Luke 1:78-79 (KJV)

My middle school English teacher would have
diagrammed this complicated sentence, the Scripture
above, with ease. She'd point out, "The meat of the
statement, subject and verb, are in the second phrase,
and the other segments answer our questions—how,
who, when, and why. But the writer begins with the
source of what is to come: the heartfelt mercies of
our God. Do you see how the author carefully
arranged everything for clarity and purpose?"

Some of us would have seen what our teacher meant.
Today, we can focus on the "How, whom, and why,"
which are questions every journalist subscribes to
answering.

"How will the sunrise break?" Through God's
heartfelt mercies.

"Upon whom will the light shine?" Us, those who sit
in darkness and death's shadow.

"Why? For what purpose?" To enlighten our steps and bring us into peace.

Allow me to illustrate my point using the Bible story about Zachariah (Luke 1:5-79). Zachariah, slow to believe the angel's prophecy that his wife would bear a son in her old age, spoke these words after his first and only child John entered the world. For nine long months, he suffered the imposition of silence, and for decades before that, had mourned the lack of children to leave behind him when he died.

Perhaps this history helped his neighbors and friends to see how momentous his visitation had been, but still, it must have been difficult for Zachariah. Finally, God's angel had promised him a son. His wife had conceived in her old age. Yet he couldn't express his excitement and joy. Bummer!

Once Zachariah agreed that his newborn son's name would be John, his tongue was loosed. At long last, it was Zachariah's turn to speak. Well aware of his imperfect faith, he'd had plenty of time to ponder what he might say at this long-awaited opportunity.

At this significant moment, a message inspired by the Holy Spirit poured forth. And what a message it was, pure poetry—pure exaltation! We might well take heed to this tale of mercy and light, drawing us from our gloomy outlook and assuring us of guidance and serenity.

Let's pray: Sometimes it's easier to fall back into familiar negativity than to embrace Your fresh light, Father. Grant us hearts to listen to Your message through Zachariah and entrust our lives to You. Deliver us from falling back from Your promises in unbelief. In Jesus's name I pray. Amen.

The Joy of Life

By Paula Moldenhauer

"Hope deferred maketh the heart sick: but when the
desire cometh, it is a tree of life."
– Proverbs 13:12 (KJV)

The birth of a child. I'll never forget the first time.
Even after seventeen hours of hard labor, little sleep,
and an aching, postpartum body, I felt fully alive—
excited, strong, and full of joy—because I held in my
arms the fulfillment of my dreams. I couldn't wait to
show off my little girl and couldn't sleep for looking
at her. I clutched her to my heart, singing to her. I
held her when she nursed, when she slept, and when
she awoke.

Perhaps the joy was more pronounced because of the
months the dream was deferred. I'll never forget the
fear, disappointment, and even anger I felt each time
I realized I wasn't pregnant during the struggle to
conceive that first baby.

Life is full of both the devastation of unrelenting
disappointment and the wild joy of dreams coming
true. Part of really living means allowing emotions on
both ends of the spectrum.

One thing I love about hanging out with the elderly is

their perspective on life. When my neighbor Bernice was almost eighty, we talked about life's struggles. She pronounced in her no-nonsense, Jewish New Yorker, mama voice, "That's just life, kid. We all have those times. Then they're over."

Bernice's philosophy was based upon experience, but in it are echoes of the Bible verse Psalm 30:5, that reminds us that weeping may last for the night, but joy comes in the morning.

My daughter, now a married woman, takes this concept a step further. She calls it living "in the and." She's learning not to stuff down the pain of life's disappointments, but at the same time to refuse to allow life's struggles to steal the joy of living. Her words remind me of my own journey to cultivate joy.

A few years ago, I had a beautiful lunch with a dear friend. She was waiting on test results concerning a serious health issue. It had her afraid and off-kilter. There were some teary moments. Yet in the midst of that pain and fear, we savored a homemade meal and good conversation. We teased and joked, our laughter ringing from the kitchen. We nursed warm cups of blueberry green tea, pausing to breathe deeply of its sweet aroma.

We embraced the "and," cultivating joy by acknowledging the beauty of life and entering into the glory of good food and fellowship without denying the struggle.

So, my friend, embrace life. Allow the seasons to ebb and flow. Cry when you need to. Laugh often. Dance in the rain when you can.

Live in the "and."

Let's pray: Father God, please help me to trust You in seasons of disappointment. When it feels overwhelming, I need Your comfort and hope. Sometimes I need help believing that joy comes in the morning, so hold me close and whisper this truth. When the crazy wonderful happens, help me believe it is real. Open my heart to enjoy every bit of the experience, and fill me with gratitude and praise. And while seasons come and seasons go, there is always the "and." I want to be real in my struggles without allowing pain to steal away the beautiful moments life offers. I want to always remember You and Your love no matter what is happening. Thank You for Your love that is never-ending. In Jesus's name I pray. Amen.

Balance

By Gail Kittleson

"Go thy way, eat thy bread with joy, and drink thy wine with a merry heart; for God now accepteth thy works. Let thy garments be always white; and let thy head lack no ointment. Live joyfully with the wife whom thou lovest all the days of the life of thy vanity, which he hath given thee under the sun, all the days of thy vanity: for that is thy portion in this life, and in thy labour which thou takest under the sun. Whatsoever thy hand findeth to do, do it with thy might; for there is no work, nor device, nor knowledge, nor wisdom, in the grave, whither thou goest."– Ecclesiastes 9:7-10 (KJV)

How do we seize life?

The key seems to be viewing each new day as a gift, even while acknowledging our struggles. We awaken with honest hearts, willing to live in the present, focusing on these twenty-four hours we've been given. On certain days of our lives, this seems almost impossible. We've all been there.

I admit it's easy to look with doubt upon folks who "dress festively" and express constant good cheer. Don't you wonder when they'll finally admit life is tough, or if they'll ever break down and show their tears? After all, no one ever instructed believers not to be human.

Once, I worked with someone who always smiled. No matter what you shared with her, she managed a cheery comeback. I began to observe her, certain her façade would eventually crack and she'd admit to having a bad day. But that never happened. Maybe we didn't work together long enough, but I still believe that deep down, she was just like the rest of us.

But what good does the opposite attitude do? Going around with a long face can be so depressing—both for us and the people around us. Why not look for the good in others and in circumstances beyond our control? After all, we all know spiritual growth seems to accelerate during the rough times.

The author of today's Scripture points to balancing our gusto with an honest recognition of the world's suffering. Not an easy task, but it's essential to maintain our equilibrium.

Perhaps that's the key: balance. Isn't much of life a study in maintaining balance? I've pondered this after a bad bout with dizziness. With my equilibrium disturbed, my most frequent prayer became, "Help!"

Without a sense of balance, poise and steadiness become pipe dreams. Accomplishing much of anything goes by the wayside. But with balance restored, we walk securely and find the energy to embrace what each day brings and enjoy our lives.

Let's pray: Dear Lord, please teach me to maintain balance in this world of ups and downs, for Your glory and for my own happiness. In Jesus's name I pray. Amen.

God's Love Letter

By Paula Moldenhauer

"That the God of our Lord Jesus Christ, the Father of glory, may give unto you the spirit of wisdom and revelation in the knowledge of him."
– Ephesians 1:17 (KJV)

I still remember the exact place it happened. Turning onto the busy street beside the mall, I pulled away from the dry cleaners. Even though it occurred almost twenty years ago, I'm reminded of the moment when I pass that location. To some, it might not seem like such a big thing but for me, it was life-changing. I listened to Christian radio as I drove with my children, who were all snug in their car seats.

And then it happened: The speaker coming across the airwaves said, "Some of you are reading the Bible as if it was a textbook, but it is actually a love letter." What?

With that one statement, my whole being woke up. The radio preacher shared truth I needed, and the Holy Spirit poked me to attention.

When you spend your life trying to be good enough, it is easy to get caught up in searching the Bible for the dos and don'ts—trying to understand what is expected rather than experiencing a relationship of love. That message on the radio was just one of many ways the Lord called to me, asking me to seek Him and not a set of behavioral guidelines.

In Ephesians 1:17, Paul prays that the Christians in Ephesus will be given the Spirit of wisdom and revelation so they can know God better. In the old days, I would have assumed we needed wisdom and revelation so we could behave appropriately, know what we are supposed to do as Christians, and win souls. But that's not what the passage says. It says we need wisdom and revelation so we can know our Lord.

Scripture tells us to get our eyes off our petty efforts to be good enough and onto the One who already is. It reminds us that Christianity isn't about our efforts and ourselves; it's about God and what He did at the cross. He gave everything to be reconciled into intimate relationship with us. Scripture invites us into the most beautiful love story of all time.

Is there any greater reason for wisdom and revelation than to know our Lord more intimately?

Let's pray: Father God, I pray for myself and my loved ones, asking, as Paul did, that You give us the Spirit of wisdom and revelation so we can know You more. I want deep, personal, and intimate insight into who You are and who Jesus is. I want to live more fully in the grandest love story of all time. In Jesus's name I pray. Amen.

Devotionals about Obedience

www.capturingtheidea.blogspot.com

Is God Arbitrary?

By Linda Wood Rondeau

"I am the Lord thy God, which have brought thee out
of the land of Egypt, out of the house of bondage."
– Exodus 20:2 (KJV)

When it came to authority, our teenage son resisted
any edict that did not mesh with his own crafted
idealism. Every rule we made resulted in endless
hours of debate. We tried to explain our rationale for
our decisions. However, discussions generally ended
with the final statement, "Because we said so. We are
your parents, and we are responsible for you. We
know things you do not. You will obey."

Eventually, he concluded resistance was futile and
acquiesced, if not from comprehension, then out of
respect for our position—and if not out of respect for
our position, then out of respect for our power.

We held the purse from which his blessings flowed.

I reminded him: My ways are not your ways.

Throughout the books of the Law, God explained His
reasons for expectations. He instituted blood
sacrifices, sin offerings, grain offerings, and wave
offerings. He specified under what conditions each

could be offered. Aaron, as the priest, was given explicit instructions on his wardrobe, his deportment, and his handling of the offerings.

In some instances, God offered explanations for His edicts. Ultimately, however, God reminded Moses who was in charge and from where the blessings flowed.

According to Leviticus 11:45 (KJV), God said, "For I am the Lord that bringeth you up out of the land of Egypt, to be your God: ye shall therefore be holy, for I am holy." He also said in Leviticus 19:37 (KJV), "Therefore shall ye observe all my statutes, and all my judgments, and do them: I am the Lord."

As we read the Law in our modern world, even the least pious among us will not argue the wisdom behind many of God's ordinances. Our knowledge of the harmful effects of bacteria lends credibility to the handling of the meat and blood following sacrifice, the confinement of persons with infectious skin diseases and discharges, avoidance of certain sexual behaviors, and the fair and just treatment of others.

These rules were intended for blessing, good health, and safety. Disobedience brought about death and disease. The Creator knows its creation and the result of its misuse.

We imperfect humans understand that our knowledge

is of a greater scope than an infant's. We make rules for our children to keep them safe, and we do this because we love them. Our decisions for the welfare of our children are not based upon their understanding or permission. We make our decisions based upon our knowledge of their individual needs and circumstances, our knowledge and experience, and the lessons we ourselves have learned from our own mistakes.

The future happiness and security of our children is our primary concern. We expect obedience even though they may not fully comprehend our reasons for the rules. How much more then, does our Heavenly Father, perfect in every way, desire good things for His children?

God's Laws are not given to cause hardship and drudgery. They are given to help us be secure in Him. When we are obedient, blessings will flow as a natural result.

According to Leviticus 26:12-13 (KJV), God said, "And I will walk among you, and will be your God, and ye shall be my people. I am the Lord your God, which brought you forth out of the land of Egypt, that ye should not be their bondmen; and I have broken the bands of your yoke, and made you go upright."

Conversely, as a natural result, disobedience will beget unpleasantness, separation, and death. In the list of calamities that God tells Moses will befall the disobedient, God warns in Leviticus 26:18 (KJV), "And if ye will not yet for all this hearken unto me, then I will punish you seven times more for your sins."

Yet even after His harsh warnings, God provides atonement for those desiring to return to Him. According to Leviticus 26:45 (KJV), He said, "But I will for their sakes remember the covenant of their ancestors, whom I brought forth out of the land of Egypt in the sight of the heathen, that I might be their God: I am the Lord."

God did not institute His Law arbitrarily. He cares for us.

Let's pray: I thank You, Lord, that You know what is best for me. I thank You that Your discipline is never arbitrary. You are Sovereign. Help me to trust You and renew my confidence as I increase in obedience. In Jesus's name I pray. Amen.

Should vs. Want

By Linda Wood Rondeau

"Howbeit when he, the Spirit of truth, is come, he
will guide you into all truth."
– John 16:13a (KJV)

I know the drill. I hear it from my doctor with every
visit. Lose weight, eat more nutritiously, and get
more exercise. After my physician has kindly
reminded me of the benefits derived from healthier
lifestyle choices, I make well-intentioned promises of
changed behaviors.

I vow to increase fiber, though to me it's not much
better than cardboard. I promise myself I will lose
fifty pounds, do aerobic activity for thirty minutes a
day, drink eight glasses of water, and consume the
requisite servings of fruits and vegetables. I pride
myself on my good intentions.

With gusto and determination, I dust off the
treadmill, put motivational stickers around the house,
and keep a diary of my new healthy ambitions. Sadly,
however, my behaviors slowly drift back to my
comfortable, unhealthy choices within a few weeks.
"I just don't have enough willpower," I tell myself
while pouring my fourth cup of coffee.

Is my inability to change due to lack of motivation? Am I too weak of spirit? I reprimand myself, asking, "Why can't I do better?"

Perhaps it is because I suffer from the "shoulds." I should drink less coffee, I should exercise more, and I should lose weight. Every magazine I pick up has more than half of its content devoted to the "shoulds."

The problem in compliance is a lack of the "wants." Oh, it's true it would be nice to be as beautiful as Miss America, as athletic as an Olympic champion, and as enthusiastic as a political candidate, but do I have the want for these things? Am I willing to make the sacrifices and commit to the long haul? My resolve wanes because I lack the "wants."

Attitudes regarding change are shaped according to whether we desire the change out of a feeling of guilt or whether the change is motivated due to a conviction. The "shoulds" are a result of guilt and the "wants" are born from conviction.

Guilt is laden with self-incrimination and self-loathing. It is a heavy burden to carry. It tends to slow progress and cause depression. Guilt may propel us into action initially, but the momentum is difficult to sustain. When we fail, we convince ourselves there is some intrinsic flaw within us that dooms us to a cycle of attempts and failures. With each failure, the desire to try again is diminished.

When we truly want to change, we are convicted toward change. Conviction alters our perspective, renews our energies, and drives us toward a positive outcome. Even if a first attempt is unsuccessful, we will keep trying until we experience ultimate success.

What about our spiritual lifestyles? We believe we should read the Bible more, attend church regularly, and give a tithe unto the Lord. Every devotional article we read reminds us of the benefits when we do these things. Yet our striving toward these goals weans as life's mundane needs erode our best intentions.

God does not desire us to follow a blind pattern of religiosity. Doing good deeds merely because one "should" do them will produce meaningless exercise that does little to uplift the believer.

God has provided the believer with the Holy Spirit. It is the Spirit's working within us that will bring the believer to conviction. He places a hunger within the believer that propels us toward God's word. Rather than condemn our past, He uses our failure as a lamp to show us what our future could be when we walk in obedience.

As we grow in our desire to walk more closely with God, we no longer pray simply because that's what a

Christian should do. We pray because our day is incomplete without spending time alone with Him.

Let's pray: Thank You, Father God, for the provision of Your Holy Spirit to draw me closer to You. Put a desire into my heart to be close to You. Help me remember—it is not so much what I do that matters most to You, but rather what is in my heart when I do those things. Forgive me when I try to serve You with wrong motivation. Take my heart, and then my hands will do what You want me to do and my feet will go where You want me to go. In Jesus's name I pray. Amen.

Come

By Gail Kittleson

"Enter into His gates with thanksgiving, and into His courts with praise: be thankful unto Him, and bless His name. For the Lord is good; His mercy is everlasting; and His truth endureth to all generations." – Psalm 100:4-5 (KJV)

What a lovely word—"come." This single syllable in the English language welcomes us and invites us to enter, to spend time with someone, to share another's company. It also invites us to follow.

I've been researching biblical references with the word "come." For example, there is come and worship—this familiar call beckons us from our fears and daily trials, from our wanderings on life's rugged byways. It provides an opportunity to lose ourselves in something bigger than us, something worthy, something that puts our sufferings into perspective.

And then there's Jesus's call to follow Him. He called men and women to do that throughout His ministry, and that following required a choice—many choices. As someone once said, "Lordship involves one big yes and a lot of little uh-huhs."

According to Mark 8:34 (KJV), Jesus said, "Whoever wants to be My disciple must deny themselves and take up their cross and follow Me."

Yes, this initial "coming" requires a choice. In choosing to come, we leave something behind at the same time. Sometimes this means, or at least feels like, sacrifice. But doesn't every decision we make in life require choosing between alternatives? Why should this be any different?

Jesus also issues another clear call to us in Matthew 11:28 (KJV) when He says, "Come unto Me, all who labour and are heavy laden, and I will give you rest."

What a wonderful promise. But this call may actually lead to more focused activity. With our need for inner rest being met by Him, we enjoy more energy to attend to our vocation, our ministry to this hurting world.

But even in this call, we are given a choice. When our children are young enough, we force them to rest, but our Heavenly Parent isn't pushy or forceful. He makes His wishes known, offers us His gifts, and waits for us to respond.

Who wouldn't accept an offer of rest? Human beings, that's who! Unfortunately, our desire to please people or to maintain control gets in the way of "come unto Him." Sometimes, it seems preferable to work ourselves into a lather rather than rest in our Savior's love.

It takes a lot of trying, trying, trying before we finally get the message about working together with God. It's like pedaling a bicycle built for two—that's why it's sometimes called the tandem bike. It only makes sense to put the partner with the greatest power in the front.

Let's pray: Please teach us, Lord, to come when You call. In Jesus's name I pray. Amen.

Following Jesus

By Melissa Henderson

"And he saith unto them, Follow me, and I will make you fishers of men."
– Matthew 4:19 (KJV)

Every time I read Scripture, I learn something new. In every life circumstance, each verse reveals something amazing and enlightening. A feeling of peace comes over me when I pick up my Bible and open the pages.

There are times when I am not searching for a particular passage. Those times, I simply open the Bible and see where the pages land. Today, the Bible opened on this Scripture in Matthew.

Matthew 4:19 gives me a reminder to look at my life and see who I am following in every moment. In this Scripture, we are told how Jesus had just begun His preaching in Galilee. He has met fishermen Simon Peter and Andrew and invites them to join Him. Jesus tells them He will make them "fishers of men."

Can you imagine the setting? Close your eyes and picture the water lapping against the side of the boat, fishermen standing while throwing their nets in and out of the water, a daily routine.

And here is Jesus, encouraging them to join Him. Did they understand His meaning of making them fishers of men? Discussion could have gone on for a while. Debates about whether they should go with Jesus or not could have occurred. Did they discuss for a long time, or did they answer quickly? Continuing to read the Bible book of Matthew, we can learn more.

If they truly became fishers of men, would they be able to bring others to Jesus? So many questions. Those fishermen had to make a decision.

Every day, we have to make a decision in our own lives. Are we going to follow Jesus and show His love to others? Or are we going to make a decision to follow someone or something else? Temptation is all around.

Making the true decision to follow Jesus allows us to show others His love through our words and actions. We never know when someone is affected by something we say or some action we take.

Perhaps while standing in the grocery line, we notice a person behind us with only one item to purchase while we have a cart full. We let that person go ahead of us. That's showing God's love.

Maybe we are taking a walk in the neighborhood and see other neighbors. We pause to say hello and have a chat. Listening and hearing to what the person shares is another way of showing God's love.

Or even in our own families, do we truly forgive and forget a wrong done to us? I have heard people say forgiving family is harder than forgiving friends. Who are we following if we don't have forgiveness in our hearts?

If we rush by opportunities to show God's love, then who are we following? Are we following material things or thinking only of ourselves? Life can be very busy, with activities, daily routines, and definitely unexpected events. Do we pause, reflect, and remember to follow the examples Jesus provided, which are love, care, and compassion? Or are we so concerned about the next minute that we move ahead without showing His love?

I pray that we will all follow Jesus each day. What a difference we could make if we became fishers of men.

Let's pray: Lord, thank You for opportunities to follow You and to share Your love with others. I pray that all my words and actions will reflect You. In Jesus's name I pray. Amen.

Don't Take It for Granted

By Quantrilla Ard

"And he said unto him, Son, thou art ever with me,
and all that I have is thine."
– Luke 15:31 (KJV)

As parents, our responsibility is to pour into our children wisdom, knowledge, and understanding. We are to teach them how to discern right from wrong and to discern between what's good and what's best. Watching them grow up and become independent thinkers is equal parts excitement and terror, as you know the challenges and difficulties that accompany this. Peer pressure, societal demands, and personal preferences all play roles in the decisions our children make. We can only hope and pray they will choose the good.

Many sermons and devotionals have drawn inspiration, taught object lessons, and mined messages of hope from Jesus's Parable of the Prodigal Son. I love this story in its entirety and in each character's story. Today, we will focus on the brother—the one who stayed behind—the one who, in my humble opinion, had the most to lose. Let's dig a little deeper into his story.

The Bible doesn't specifically go into the historical

details of this family. Honestly, I've always wondered where the mother was! We are only afforded a snapshot in time of this hypothetical family: a hard-working father and his sons.

One son, tired of his daily duties and ready to make it on his own, asks for his inheritance and leaves home. We know how the story goes—he loses all he owns and returns home destitute and apologetic. The father is moved with compassion for his son and welcomes him home with open arms and celebration.

The other son, the one left at home, broods over his father's reaction to his brother's return. The parable doesn't discuss what this son did while his brother was away. However, he is left at home to help the father as his choice was made for him once his brother decided to leave. Someone had to stay behind.

I'm not sure if there was an actual invitation from the other brother to leave, but many of us can relate to him in regards to having your circumstances dictated by the behavior and decisions of someone else. It doesn't seem fair, and if our emotions are unchecked, the root of bitterness can take hold in our hearts and lives.

Here are a few areas in which I believe the brother who stayed at home lost sight of the prize: He viewed being at home with his father as a punishment rather than a blessing. He resented his brother for leaving but didn't show him grace when he returned. He focused on the external blessings his brother received and did not recognize the internal change that had taken place in his life. He viewed his brother as being selfish for leaving but didn't himself take advantage of his father's best qualities: forgiveness and compassion.

How could this brother have lived with his father and worked beside him all those years and not reflect his character? Sound familiar yet?

How can we, who know the character of our Heavenly Father and have spent time with Him, not reflect His character? Why do we question God when good things seem to happen for others while we have waited in His Presence with our hands outstretched? Have we, too, taken our relationship with the Father for granted by allowing ourselves to be in His presence but letting the roots of bitterness and lack of compassion permeate our lives?

What the brother failed to recognize is that the father would have just as readily given him whatever he asked for. All the father had belonged to him, as well.

Friends, let's draw close to our Father not in hopes of what we will receive as a reward, but because we love Him and want His character to be reproduced in us. And because He is such a good Father, He will sing and rejoice over us also when we come to ourselves and return to Him. Let's desire the Giver more than the gifts He gives.

Let's pray: Sometimes it's easy for me to lose sight of Your love for me God, because I'm too busy trying to earn it. Thank You for showing me through this parable that I can do nothing to either earn or diminish that love. Like the Parable of the Prodigal Son, help me to turn back to You if I ever wander from You. Like the son who stayed, help me to find my security in Your forgiveness and mercy, never to be a slave to comparison. I belong to You, and that is enough. In Jesus's name I pray. Amen.

Alexis A. Goring

Devotionals about Forgiveness

www.capturingtheidea.blogspot.com

Don't Nurse It. Don't Rehearse It. Let It Go.

By Nanci Rubin

"And herein do I exercise myself, to have always a conscience void of offense toward God, and toward men." – Acts 24:16 (KJV)

I cannot tell you how much time I've spent looking in the rearview mirror of my life and questioning why God didn't answer my prayers.

I have been so myopic over the hairline fractures in my life that I was blinded to what God had for me. There was a season where it seemed every sermon I heard dealt with past offenses and forgiveness. It took me over a year before I got it!

You cannot see where God is leading when you're looking backward. I can see now how God had things He wanted to get to me, but I was too dumb to receive them and beyond stubborn to forgive, which would have enabled me so I could.

When one is betrayed, it opens one up for a tremendous propensity to not forgive and to become a martyr. I kept the pain of my betrayal hidden, or so I thought. I absolutely refused to give it up. It was my pain and I reveled in it. In the midnight hour, I would rehearse the pain over and over. Sometimes I mentally plotted revenge. I had imaginary conversations with my betrayer that I could never have had in reality.

Somehow these nighttime scrimmages lent a measure of relief from the continuous pain I lived with. Make no mistake—betrayal is toxic. Unforgiveness is unhealthy, and it kept me tied to the one I had been hurt by. Until I was willing to confess my unforgiveness and pray a blessing over those who had hurt me did I finally have peace over the pain of betrayal. I was stuck in my own misery.

We have to be mindful of the necessity of forgiveness. In Matthew 6:15 (KJV) Jesus said, "But if ye forgive not men their trespasses, neither will your Father forgive your trespasses." He couldn't have said it any simpler: We are compelled to forgive. It's not an option; we need to do it.

We must be careful not to say we won't forgive someone. I had a pastor many years ago, a wonderful man of God, married to an anointed woman gifted with a music ministry. The church prospered under their leadership, and God was blessing it.

Then overnight, it all fell apart. The pastor's wife had an affair with one of the deacons, but to add insult to injury, it was the pastor's best friend. He could have chosen to not forgive her, but he didn't. He did not become embittered. Everyone in the church was in total awe of his ability to forgive.

Revenge not only lowers you to your betrayer's lowest level—what's worse, it boomerangs. One who seeks revenge is like a fool who shoots himself in order to hit his enemy with the kick of the gun's recoil.

Revenge is the most worthless weapon in the world. It ruins the avenger, all the while confirming the enemy in the wrongdoing. All of this is the beginning of a root of bitterness. And what strange things bitterness can do to us. It slowly sets, like a permanent plaster cast, perhaps protecting the wearer from further pain but ultimately holding the sufferer rigid in frozen animation. Feelings and responses turn to concrete. Bitterness is paralysis.

Bitterness is a cyclical, repetitive, tightly closed circle of self-centered pain. It carries us around and around the same senseless arc, around and around ourselves. Like a child learning to ride a bicycle, knowing how to ride but not how to stop, we pedal on and on, afraid to quit, yet wishing desperately for someone to come and take the handlebars, break our circling, and let us off.

Bitterness is useless. Repayment is impossible. Revenge is impotent. Resentment is impractical.

Only forgiveness can reconcile the differences and restore healing to a relationship. God knew that we could not hold to offenses because offenses will eventually take hold of us.

God said we must forgive, and in doing so we can receive healing. Let's not hold offenses and be locked to the past. Let go and allow God to intervene.

Let's pray: Our Father in Heaven, who could have been more offended than You? You sent Your Son for sinful humanity, and He was not received. Yet You took no offense but loved us anyway. Thank You! In Jesus's name I pray. Amen.

How to Be Abundantly Free

By Paula Moldenhauer

"In whom we have redemption through his blood, the
forgiveness of sins, according to the riches of his
grace; Wherein he hath abounded toward us in all
wisdom and prudence."
– Ephesians 1:7-8 (KJV)

Because of Christ's sacrifice, we are abundantly free.
Free from our imperfections. Free from our guilt.
Free from the constant demand to "live up" to
unrealistic standards.

Let me paint a picture of freedom. Many years ago
when I was a young mother, my kids and I had a
really bad day. I was unkind. Mean even. And then I
felt awful! Shocked by the pain in their precious
eyes, I gave myself a timeout—only it wasn't a
healthy one.

Instead of confessing to the Lord my shortcomings
and accepting His forgiveness, I wallowed in self-
loathing. I hated the way I acted and felt I didn't
deserve His grace. I couldn't forgive myself. In the
more distant past, I would have wallowed in guilt for
days. But praise be to God for His marvelous grace,
as He'd begun breaking that cycle within me. I was
growing in my ability to understand that since Christ

took my sins upon Himself, and I was covered by His righteousness, I could live a life without condemnation, even during my failings. The Bible says, "There is therefore now no condemnation to them which are in Christ Jesus, who walk not after the flesh, but after the Spirit." (Romans 8:1)

The happy ending of that hard day is that I cried out to the Lord to help me, and He did.

My emotions calmed. I went to my children and asked their forgiveness. Then an amazing thing happened. My oldest son, then about ten years old, ministered to me. I don't remember what scriptures he spoke that day. I only know they were led by the Holy Spirit, and they offered God's heart of forgiveness.

Soon, all four children and I piled up together. We forgave each other, ordered a pizza, and watched a movie.

It was over. Just like that.

And that is freedom.

Relationship. Forgiveness. Moving on.

If you ever are tempted to punish yourself when you blow it, please consider this: Christ died so we could have forgiveness. He took our punishment upon

Himself. He doesn't want us to penalize ourselves. Scripture says He didn't come to condemn the world, but to save it (John 3:17). He took our life of failings upon the cross and replaced it with the perfect and complete freedom to enjoy His grace.

As I'm learning to rest in the grace of Jesus, there's a beautiful side effect. God is changing me into His image. I'm still not perfect. But as I accept the gift of salvation that Jesus Christ offers, some of the old junk I struggled with is simply dropping away.

Won't you join me, my precious friend in Christ, in accepting the abundant freedom of God's grace?

Let's pray: Dear Jesus, thank You for the deliverance and salvation that comes through Your blood. Your gift of forgiveness, the remission of our shortcomings and trespasses, is an example of the generosity of Your gracious favor. Empower us to walk in the freedom of Your grace. In Jesus's name I pray. Amen.

God's Unmerited Favor

By Nanci Rubin

"For by grace are ye saved through faith; and not of yourselves: it is the gift of God: Not of works lest any man should boast." – Ephesians 2:8-9 (KJV)

This Scripture always pings my heart. I try to envision God in Heaven asking, "Who will go and save My creation? My children have been deceived and have gotten off course. They need someone to show them the way home, someone who can bridge the crevasse sin has created."

I can imagine the angels, the Holy Spirit, and Jesus Christ talking with God at a heavenly board meeting. Jesus, the chairman of International Outreach, raises His hand and says, "I will go." Everyone nods, and an ethereal melody that only the Heavenly Host can hear permeates the atmosphere. The angels nominate Jesus as God's representative, and the Holy Spirit seconds the motion. Everyone is in agreement. God's only begotten son will become the Savior of the world.

There is a flurry of activity as preparations are made for Jesus to come to earth as the Son of Man. He willingly laid aside His robe and crown to come down to our level. He became the propitiation for our sins. I often wonder why He did that. How deep is a love that would willingly take all our afflictions and sins? It is beyond all human comprehension.

So how does grace come into this? Ephesians 2:8-9 states that we're saved by grace, God's unmerited favor, not by anything we say or can do. Salvation is God's greatest gift to mankind. He gives it freely. We can't earn it. We can't save ourselves. We all need a Savior, and God knew it. It wasn't enough any longer for our sins to be merely covered by the blood of a sacrificial animal. It was time for our sins to be washed away, once and for all. The plan of salvation was accomplished by the blood that Jesus shed when He died at Calvary. His sacrifice opened the door unto eternal life.

In Isaiah 53, God's Word clearly defines what Jesus accomplished for us at The Cross. He took all of our sins upon Himself and died in our place so that we may be saved in God's Kingdom. Sometimes, I believe we fail to understand this gift of grace.

I want to have the unmerited favor of God. I want to know that when I fail and sin, which we all do, that God has made a way for me, and you, to confess our sins and be forgiven. We need to get it through our heads that God loves us so much that He has given all He can to show us His love. There is not one thing you can do to make Him love you more, nor can you do anything to make Him love you less. He just loves you.

God wants to restore you back into fellowship with Him. We all have such a tendency to run from God when we've messed up, but we should be running to Him.

This is the walk we choose when we accept grace. It's wonderful to know God is always there and ready to restore us when we've gotten off course. Don't allow the enemy to deceive you into believing God will not forgive you. Remember God's Grace and Jesus Christ's sacrifice for you.

If by chance you've stumbled and lost your way, call out to God and tell Him you're sorry and want His unmerited favor. When our children err and confess what they've done, we forgive them because we love them. God loves you a zillion more times than you love your children. Remember that truth, and let your life be forever changed.

Let's pray: Dear Father in Heaven, I do not have enough words to thank You for the gift of Your grace, Your unmerited favor. Help us to see ourselves the way You see us. In Jesus's name I pray. Amen.

Devotionals about A New Start

www.capturingtheidea.blogspot.com

Change and the New Year

By Gail Kittleson

"But we all, with open face beholding as in a glass
the glory of the Lord, are changed into the same
image from glory to glory, even as by the Spirit of
the Lord."
– 2 Corinthians 3:18 (KJV)

Looking back over the decades gives me pause.
Especially as I approach December 31 and January 1,
I find myself in a reflective mood revolving around a
word I resist: change.

This word appears in the passage above as a strong
verb. The New King James Version of the Holy Bible
translates "change" as "transform." But the "by"
remains the same, signaling the passive voice.

Passive? How can we be passive facing a new year?

Normally on New Year's, I spend time reflecting on
the past 365 days and do some journaling and list-
writing. What areas should I work on in the coming
year?

In recent years, I devote more time to giving thanks
for all the ways God has blessed and guided me
during the year, rather than wallowing in regret over

my failures. That signifies progress, because all these years of trying to "walk the walk" have taught me that whatever true change occurs in me comes by grace rather than by my own efforts.

We all know about the earth-shattering discovery of penicillin during World War II that saved countless soldiers' lives.

In 1945, Sir Alexander Fleming, Ernst Boris Chain, and Sir Howard Walter Florey won the Nobel Prize in physiology in medicine. Penicillin's curative effect on various infectious diseases changed the world forever.

But here's an interesting angle: Nearly seventy-five years later, doctors still say, "Take the whole course of antibiotics." These instructions stem from Alexander Fleming's belief, but modern research now challenges this idea, and many physicians believe taking the entire course of antibiotics is unwise.

With no medical expertise, I wouldn't lobby for one action or the other, but it's interesting to consider how difficult change can be, even in the scientific world. I can easily understand transformation being difficult in relationships, but since science is devoted to the study of alterations in nature and our society, I assume there would be less clinging to tradition.

It's only human to cling to the way we've always been and always done things. While it's easy to pray, "Change me, Lord," it is much more difficult to live through those changes, and especially to allow God to choose what it is that needs to be transformed.

Reflecting on today's Scripture, I believe I need to adopt the "Show Me" motto: "God, show me what You want."

Let's pray: Dear Lord of change and circumstance, grant me courage to embrace what You want for me. Help me to remember that You love me and long for me to become more like Your Son. In Jesus's Name I pray. Amen.

A Fresh Start

By Jessica Brodie

"Wherefore henceforth know we no man after the flesh: yea, though we have known Christ after the flesh, yet now henceforth know we him no more. Therefore if any man be in Christ, he is a new creature: old things are passed away; behold, all things are become new. And all things are of God, who hath reconciled us to himself by Jesus Christ, and hath given to us the ministry of reconciliation; To wit, that God was in Christ, reconciling the world unto himself, not imputing their trespasses unto them; and hath committed unto us the word of reconciliation."
– 2 Corinthians 5:16-19 (KJV)

Do you remember that first-day-of-school feeling?

Not the butterfly-fluttery, heart-thump jitters about who your teacher is or whether you'll make any friends, but that giddy-specialness kind of feeling: new spiral notebooks, pages all fresh and clean. Rows of sharpened pencils and slick, brand-new pens. Stacks of notebook paper gleaming in their plastic wrappers. Binders with their three shiny rings ready to be filled.

Everything ready. A clean start.

That's how I feel about Mondays, or the first day of a new month, or New Year's Day—no matter what the week, month, or year prior might have brought, good or bad, it is a day of beginning. It's a chance to start anew, an opportunity to begin on the right foot. It's like I'm getting my very own different-colored spiral notebook with crisp blank pages just waiting for their scribbles and wisdom, only I get to live it.

If the week, month, or year prior has been a good one, I'm excited to keep riding that proverbial high and sail along with God to the next level. If it's been meh or downright awful, I get to set it aside like that finally finished project, turn my head, and cast my eyes on the next adventure.

Yes, adventure—whatever our situation, whatever our condition, whatever our joy or grief or pain or illness or worry, a new start is a new adventure, and if we wrap our minds around it correctly and look at it in what I like to call the "God light," it's absolutely, magnificently glorious.

See, I take to heart the Scripture above, particularly verse 17, which says, "Therefore, if anyone is in Christ, the new creation has come: The old has gone, the new is here."

In Christ, I am a new creation. A new week or month or year is yet another opportunity to celebrate that.

If we look deeper at that chapter, we see that verse is part of God's larger point: His ministry of reconciliation, of fresh starts, of bridge-building, wall-falling and barrier-breaking. We are urged to put on our God lenses, to view "no one from a worldly point of view" (verse 16).

After all, as we are told above, God "reconciled us to Himself through Christ ... not counting people's sins against them." The old has gone. All the sin is washed away. All we need to do is be reconciled—reunited in peaceful, beautiful harmony—with God, and we get to share in that.

The new is here. Literally and figuratively.

Every day is a new opportunity to walk in the light of God, to walk with Him, to let Him work His wonders and plans through us. He has big plans for us, and those plans can fly free and soar if we just step aside and make room for God.

That's the catch, and sometimes it takes constant work to remember it: We are most certainly not in this alone. Our very existence is not only smoother and happier but fully in line with the Lord and His glory when we realize that. Our steps are not our own. They are steps with our Creator if we only take a moment to stop fighting Him like an independence-craving toddler and let Him light the way.

May your fresh new spiral notebook be God-colored, God-inspired, and God-led. The old has gone. The new is here.

Let's pray: Father God, sometimes we are so fixated on the past that we allow it to define us or shape our expectation of the future. But in You, we are new, fresh, clean, and pure. In You we are a new creation. Help us push aside the pain, disappointments, and sins of our past to embrace our present and future at Your feet. In Jesus's name I pray. Amen.

The Newness of You

By Glynis Becker

"Therefore if any man be in Christ, he is a new creature: old things are passed away; behold, all things are become new."
– 2 Corinthians 5:17 (KJV)

I believe in the new creation that Christ is working in me. I believe in my head that I have been made new, that I am different than I was before I began a life that followed Christ and allowed the Holy Spirit to guide, direct, and comfort me.

But sometimes I have a hard time believing it in my heart.

I've been a believer for a long time. I grew up in a Christian home. I've been in church nearly every week of my entire middle-aged life. I accepted Jesus and made a commitment to him when I was just seven years old.

Although my parents will confirm that I wasn't a perfect teenager, I never felt the need to rebel against the confines of my faith during those tough years that stretch us into the adult we will become. I've pretty much been the poster child for the term "good girl" my whole life.

And it might sound surprising, but I often have to remind myself this is not a bad thing.

Here's what I mean: Because I never seemed to stray very far from the path Christ has for me, I am easily lulled into believing two very dangerous lies. The first lie is that I have somehow saved myself. And the second is that I didn't need saving in the first place.

Why are these lies so dangerous? Because if left unchecked, they lead to self-righteousness toward people and apathy toward the great gift of salvation we've been given when we accept Jesus Christ and believe in Him. If we begin to believe we have the ability to save ourselves, then we also easily find ourselves looking down on others. How arrogant and unloving we can become if we think others should be saving themselves, as well!

And what happens if we get the idea that we didn't need to be saved in the first place? We will lose the awe, wonder, reverence, and weight of the enormous sacrifice God gave us through Jesus. May we never take that for granted!

Since the beginning of creation, God has been doing new and miraculous things in the lives of His people. Do you remember what He told the Israelites?

God said in Isaiah 43:18-19 (KJV), "Remember ye not the former things, neither consider the things of old. Behold, I will do a new thing; now it shall spring forth; shall ye not know it? I will even make a way in the wilderness, and rivers in the desert."

I believe that promise still holds true for us. Isn't it exciting to know God is at work all over the world and in each of our lives all the time?

So do you feel new today? Maybe not, but remind yourself that God is constantly—daily, hourly, and moment-by-moment—working in your life, if you give him the space to do so. You can and should be different today, even in a tiny way, than you were yesterday.

Remember to have grace with those around you, as Christ works in their lives, as well.

And may we always remember this verse in Galatians 2:20 (KJV): "I am crucified with Christ: nevertheless I live; yet not I, but Christ liveth in me: and the life which I now live in the flesh I live by the faith of the Son of God, who loved me, and gave himself for me."

Let's pray: Thank You, Father God, for the gift of a new heart, a new mind, and a new purpose that mirrors Jesus's redemptive work in this world. Let me see with fresh eyes the gift You have given me and help me to lovingly share that gift and that grace with those around me. In Jesus's name I pray. Amen.

Springtime: God's CPR

By Nanci Rubin

"While the earth remaineth, seedtime and harvest, and cold and heat, and summer and winter, and day and night shall not cease." – Genesis 8:22 (KJV)

In February, you'll find me pouring through the Burpee seed catalog in anticipation of spring planting as God makes preparation to perform cardio-pulmonary resuscitation and revive the earth from its winter repose. Nothing excites me more than to see crocuses as they emerge through the snow-covered earth and the unforgettable sweet aroma of lavender and pink hyacinths heralding rebirth. It's nature fulfilling God's promise as found in Genesis.

To me, gardening epitomizes seedtime and harvest and brings Scripture to life. After many years of planting my garden, I can safely say you reap what you sow. If I plant green beans, I don't expect to harvest beets. It's the same in our daily lives. What seed are you sowing? Envy? Strife? Mercy? Love? Forgiveness?

Every spring, as the earth goes through rebirth, I am reminded of the born-again experience. As my seedlings sprout, I remember the parable Jesus offered in Matthew 13:4-8 (KJV) about the sower sowing the seed: "And when he sowed, some seeds fell by the way side, and the fowls came and devoured them up: Some fell upon stony places, where they had not much earth: and forthwith they sprung up, because they had no deepness of earth: And when the sun was up, they were scorched; and because they had no root, they withered away. And some fell among thorns; and the thorns sprung up, and choked them: But other fell into good ground, and brought forth fruit, some an hundredfold, some sixtyfold, some thirtyfold."

It's very interesting as a gardener to read about how the seed (the Word of God) was sown in different types of soil. The soil makes all the difference in your garden. I cultivate the soil and I add nutrients when needed. My seedlings without good soil won't develop to their expected potential. It's the same for us as new creations. God has called us. He has forgiven us, has written His Word on our hearts, and desires for us to grow. It is up to us to cultivate and guard the seed sown in our hearts.

After you've received Jesus in your heart, the enemy will come immediately to destroy that which has been sown. He'll accuse you, remind you of your past, and beat you down with his weapons of mass destruction. His attacks are individualized as we tell him our fears. We talk too much. Social media has become the enemy's new battleground.

Most of us have purchased indoor plants or outdoor scrubs. They all come with instructions on care, how we are to nourish them and keep them alive. God has done the same for us. He's given us His instruction manual, His Word (the Holy Bible). Read it. Let it water your soul, nourish your body, and give you direction. It is the fertilizer you need to grow up in Him.

Last summer, I experienced an infestation of Japanese beetles of biblical proportion. Nothing I used worked. I had to hand pick every single one. It took me weeks. The beetle fiasco reminded me how we should never allow our hearts to become hardened and immune to the Word of God.

As I handpicked those beetles, I thought about God's Word and how much the enemy hates it. He desires to infest our minds with his lies, pulling at us so he can divert us from God's plan. However, no matter what he says or does, the enemy can never pluck you from God's Hand.

Your mistakes don't cancel God's plan in your life. He's planted you in the orchard of His Heart. You're the apple of His eye, and He loves you.

Bloom where you're planted.

Let's pray: Dear Father in Heaven, how precious is Your Word. Help us to mature and grow with strong roots grounded in a firm foundation. In Jesus's name we pray. Amen.

Surrender to the Master Gardener

By Paula Moldenhauer

"I am the true vine, and my Father is the husbandman. Every branch in me that beareth not fruit he taketh away: and every branch that beareth fruit, he purgeth it, that it may bring forth more fruit."
– John 15:1-2 (KJV)

The snip-snip of scissors punctuated the tiny ache I felt as the blossoms, now faded and drawn, toppled to the ground, scattering pastel petals across the concrete of my driveway.

It was necessary to cut away the old blossoms so new ones could quickly replace them, but it was hard to let go of the glory of that rosebush, which now stood taller than my head. Never had it been as beautiful, and never had it produced so many flowers. Those sixty-plus roses, lying in clusters at my feet, seemed to whisper a truth I didn't want to think about.

I gathered handful after handful of fading blossoms and tossed them into the trash. I struggled not to mourn too deeply at their passing.

Glancing back at the bush, a bit of satisfaction pushed away the loss. The bush now looked fresh and vibrant. Newly budding roses popped out, no longer hiding behind fading flowers.

My life, too, has had many blossoms I thought would live forever—jobs I've done, friendships that grew, talents I discovered. And yet many times they opened up, let off their beautiful fragrance, showed their moments of glory, and were then cut away.

Yet I remained, pruned and shaped with room for new blossoms.

There is perhaps no greater analogy in my life than my recent steps into an empty nest. Letting each child go and become his or her own rosebush includes loss. I miss them. I miss my role in their journey. I let go of directing and soothing and teaching. I allow distance where I long for closeness. As I hear the snip of time's pruning shears, I begin to see new blooms. Relationships slowly shift from mom-in-charge to mom-held-at-arm's-length to mom-as-friend. My schedule that once was crammed full of children opens up with space to more fully become me. A marriage that was strongly child-focused discovers the joy in being two-focused again.

Each of life's blooms is glorious.

I long to tell the young to embrace every bloom the Good Lord sees fit to produce in them, to stretch to the Son and let that flower grow to its full potential, bringing joy to all who delight in such beauty and perfume. I want to encourage them to also allow the Master Gardener to cut away blossoms at His will. He alone knows which buds need space to grow and open to the Light and which old blossoms are hindering new growth.

Come to think of it, this blossom cycle continues forever. Like the rosebush that produces season after season, there will always be buds, full blooms, and fading flowers. We need only the grace to surrender to the Master Gardener to be a rosebush that flourishes, always full of blossoms.

Let's pray: Lord, help me to enjoy the blossoms in this season of life. I surrender to Your shears, willing to change as new seasons come into my life. Give me excitement for the buds. Prune me and shape me so that I can consistently produce beautiful, fragrant offerings to You. In Jesus's name I pray. Amen.

A Call to Life

By Paula Moldenhauer

"The thief cometh not, but for to steal, and to kill,
and to destroy: I am come that they might have life,
and that they might have it more abundantly."
– John 10:10 (KJV)

"Life and death are only a split second apart."

My husband said those words from his bed in the
intensive care unit of a hospital.

My thoughts agreed with his statement, for I'd nearly
lost my husband.

There is no exaggeration in this. The main artery to
the heart, the "widow maker," had been ninety-nine
percent closed. As the ambulance blared its way to
the hospital, everything was fading to black. He
prayed, "Lord, if You're taking me now, please be
with Paula and the children. It's going to be very hard
on them."

Instead of that final covering of darkness, he heard
the EMT yelling, "Jerry! Stay with me."

God intervened, and modern medicine intervened.
Since that scary event, my husband, Jerry, has

recovered. The days spent at the hospital are already fading into memory. Now we live.

I like how John 10:10 reads in the New Living Translation of the Holy Bible, in which Jesus says, "My purpose is to give them a rich and satisfying life."

When you think about that word, "life," is there anything more satisfying than our God? Doesn't the richest, fullest life begin and end in Jesus?

Jesus tells us in John 14:6 (KJV) that He is life, saying, "I am the way, the truth, and the life: no man cometh unto the Father, but by me." I understood Jesus as "the way" when I was about seven. I heard that to live with God forever, you had to accept Jesus as your Savior, so I did.

I've known Him as the truth since my early thirties. Before then, "truth" was a tiny set of doctrine that was exclusive to my particular brand of religion. Jesus did away with that kind of thinking, showing me He is Truth with a capital T. That simple but profound understanding took my life to a whole new level. I quit focusing on a "small truth" to-do list and began focusing on Jesus. It changed everything.

And finally, I've experienced Jesus as "the life."

When Jesus is our life, relationship with Him

becomes integral to who we are and everything we experience. As we surrender to Jesus as our life, He ushers us into a grand adventure of relationship with Him, astounding self-discovery, and living as His beloved.

Jesus wants to give us the most robust life possible, the life only He offers. Jesus didn't only come as the entrance into a relationship with God (the way). Nor did He only come as the One who sets us free by love (the truth), but He also came as the One who becomes our all (the life). This life that He is offers a doorway into new, abundant living. Jesus came that we could have life and have it to the fullest.

I've only dipped my big toe in the ocean of life in Him. Much of it has been crazy-wonderful. Some of it is breathtakingly scary! He's taught me much that changed the trajectory of my life and the life I give to my family. He's given me adventure and courage and unconditional, joyful love. Still, that rich, satisfying relationship with Him as my life doesn't mean everything has been easy.

Maybe you're thinking your day doesn't feel rich, satisfying, full, or abundant. I get it. I mean hospitals and near-death experiences aren't exactly fun. The first day home from the hospital, I felt like Jell-O. It was amazing how exhausting the four days had been, from the heart attack to Jerry's return home. But even those days of ambulances, stents, and heart monitors were about life—a life possible only because God ordained it.

It doesn't take a heart attack to know God is the sustainer of life, but a near-death experience certainly brings it to the front of our thinking. My friend, you and I (and my husband) are here because God chose us to live, to experience life with Him.

Let's pause and ask Him to help us receive life as He wants to give it.

Let's pray: Dear Jesus, please help me to discover You as my very life, a life grounded in love. I want to enjoy this gift of life You've given, even on the hard days. Draw me closer to You so I may release my burdens and walk with You in a trusting and joyful relationship. Show me who You really are and how to live in abundance and satisfaction. In Jesus's name I pray. Amen.

Alexis A. Goring

Devotionals about God's Love for You

God Cares

By Nanci Rubin

"Not forsaking the assembling of yourself together, as the manner some is; but exhorting one another, and so much the more, as ye see the day approaching." – Hebrews 10:25 (KJV)

"Does God care?"

I can't tell you how many times I've asked that question. But I can unequivocally say, "Yes, He does!"

When we're hurting and we can't see beyond our pain, His Word brings hope. But in the times when our pain is constant and unrelenting, then the assembling of ourselves with one another becomes a healing balm. When our church family is interceding on our behalf, healing can begin. There is no family like the family of God. We need one another.

I have so many friends who have been wounded and silently sit on the sidelines no longer willing to enter a church. Their reasons are their own. I have survived two church splits in my lifetime—neither was pretty, and they left wounds that lasted a long time. Healing comes, but as with all things, it came in God's time.

I'm grateful I didn't become bitter. I have a couple of friends who never entered a church again. They have chosen to embrace their pain, to nurse it and rehearse it. The past holds them frozen in time. They no longer trust any ministry. It saddens me to see the wounded remain victims. God created a family, and we complete each other. I pray my friends will trust again and allow God to bring them to an area in which they are willing to be healed. We need to keep our eyes on Jesus. Men will fail, but He never will.

I was reading a book recently conveying how many born-again Christians are the children of God but have never become acquainted with our Father. It's an interesting topic and one I have never considered.

I think a lot of us don't realize how interested He is in each of us individually (not just as a group, or a body, or a church). He is interested in each of His children, and He loves every single one with the same love. I've also read that often our relationship with our earthly fathers creates an atmosphere of how we perceive our Heavenly Father. It is difficult for those of us who have had absentee fathers, abusive fathers, or harsh and cold fathers to see our Heavenly Father as the loving, caring Father He is.

In the Old Testament, after the tabernacle was built first and the temple second, they didn't know Him as Father God. They knew Him as Elohim, or Jehovah. They did not know Him personally.

The enemy doesn't want you to know God's love. He wants to beat you down and tell you your sin is too great and you can't be forgiven. He makes you remember the ugliness of your sinful past before coming to Jesus.

But God is not mad at you, He is mad about you! His love for you is so great there is nothing on earth to compare it to. God is love. When we've committed sins and remain in isolation from our guilt, this will eventually cause us to feel He's not here or He doesn't care.

The ruse of the enemy is to alienate us from our Father, but all we have to do is repent, confess we've missed the mark, ask for forgiveness, and move on. We're all sinners saved by grace.

God is not holding a big stick to wield across your back. Jesus made a way for us to cross the chasm of sin and come back to fellowship with Him. We must learn to see ourselves as God does. He sees us as the finished product of love, complete and whole.

Don't be down on yourself, for God loves you just the way you are. He'll hide you under the shadow of His wings when you need healing, He'll carry you when you can't walk, He'll fight your battles for you, and He'll never leave nor forsake you.

It is a privilege to be in service to the King. Blessings to you all.

Let's pray: Heavenly Father, I pray for the lost, the hurting, those who do not know You as Father, and those who have never known an earthly Father. Bring them comfort in Jesus's name I pray. Amen.

God's Love is Stronger than a Mother's Love

By Jessica Brodie

"Can a woman forget her sucking child, that she
should not have compassion on the son of her womb?
yea, they may forget, yet will I not forget thee.
Behold, I have graven thee upon the palms of my
hands; thy walls are continually before me."
– Isaiah 49:15-16 (KJV)

It's a five-by-five booklet of vanilla construction
paper, folded and stapled just so, and it's one of the
most precious things I possess.

Titled "About Mom," my teenage son, Cameron,
crafted it for me when he was about six, probably for
Mother's Day. The booklet consists of eighteen
pages, each with a single sentence on each page
written in pencil in what was his very best
handwriting:

Thank you for everything.
You are so nice and sweet.
I love you so much.
I will behave every day.
You mean a lot to me.
I love your eyes and your heart.
I will never be mean to you ever again.

You are not mean.
You are sweet and pretty.
I will not give you a mean look.

I love red because you love it.
You do not do anything wrong.
If I were you, I would be bad.
I would protect you.
I would give them a punch, a kick butt.

I hope you're safe.
That's why you should stay out of danger.

Cameron is my oldest, the boy who made me a mom in the first place, and his sensitive and fierce soul is reflected in each of those pages—his valiant small-boy pledge to protect me from danger, his promise to behave, his insistence that he'll never be mean to me or give me a mean look, his flattery, his sweet words. I look at him now, feet taller and almost fourteen, and can still hear those words pour from his lips, still know he meant them with every ounce of his being.

We're close now, Cameron and I, but I know things are changing in his world. He's in eighth grade now, and soon he'll be in high school, then college. He'll meet the woman of his dreams and start a family. I hope and pray we'll be just as close as the years pass, hope that I'll be able to love and know his wife and his children, hope that I'll see him grow old, become even more wise and mature and kind. I have so many dreams for this child, now and far into the future.

Is that what God thinks when He looks at us, I wonder? He hears our prayers in the lonely night or the stillness of dawn, heartfelt and pleading, and knows we mean them completely. He hopes we'll stay close to Him, hopes we'll remember Him, though He understands—even if He doesn't much like it—when the distractions of life pull us here and there and far from Him. Still, He is there, His love unchanging and unfailing, His heart soaring when we return.

That love is sometimes unbelievable to us. We feel guilt about our sins, guilt that we turned from our Lord. We fear He will reject or forget us.

Never! God tells us through His prophet, Isaiah: "Can a woman forget her sucking child, that she should not have compassion on the son of her womb? yea, they may forget, yet will I not forget thee. Behold, I have graven thee upon the palms of my hands; thy walls are continually before me." (Isaiah 49:15-16 KJV).

God loves us even more than a mother loves her children. His love is more than words, more than a life stage, more than a promise. It's a covenant, a seal, a truth we can count on for always. The Bible says, "For God so loved the world, that he gave his only begotten Son, that whosoever believeth in him should not perish, but have everlasting life." (John 3:16 KJV).

As consuming and powerful as they are to me, the dreams I have for my sweet son can't hold a candle to the dreams God has for us, His children. Those dreams include eternal life! Life forever, with Him! We are blessed beyond measure.

Today, I hope you love the people in your world—whether children, spouse, family, or friends—with all your heart. Remember that however strong that love is, God's love for us is ever stronger. Forever!

Let's pray: Father God, it's so beautiful to see Your love displayed in such innocence. Thank You for loving us. Thank You for sending Your Son. Help us to love as You love us. In Jesus's name I pray. Amen.

Holy Kisses

By Paula Moldenhauer

"Let him kiss me with the kisses of his mouth: for thy love is better than wine. Because of the savour of thy good ointments thy name is as ointment poured forth, therefore do the virgins love thee. Draw me, we will run after thee: the king hath brought me into his chambers: we will be glad and rejoice in thee, we will remember thy love more than wine: the upright love thee."
– Song of Solomon 1:2-4 (KJV)

The church hymn "Burdens Are Lifted at Calvary," by John M. Moore, always makes me feel a strong sense of the Lord's care for me whenever I hear it. One morning, it played in my heart as I woke.

The day before had held one minor disaster after the next, and I'd been discouraged, but now Jesus felt close. His presence gave me the confidence to face another day.

According to pastor and speaker Mike Bickle, I experienced a divine kiss. He writes that the divine kiss is a metaphor for intimacy with Christ, and those special moments we share are like kisses from the Groom to His bride—a divine blessing that is better than anything else life has to offer. Bickle gets this idea from Song of Solomon 1:2, which says, "Let him kiss me with the kisses of his mouth: for thy love is better than wine."

There are a lot of things in life I enjoy: flowers, children's laughter, a new dress, a long walk with my man, pretty things, and happy moments. But it really is true that the very deepest and best things in life are the kisses of the Bridegroom.

Some of the worst, most painful times have also been the best because my Bridegroom's love was tangible. Attention from the Divine is better than anything mortal.

I love how the bride in the Song of Solomon begs her groom to kiss her "again and again." She knows she needs His repeated attention. She craves intimacy. She longs to be held so close to her King that she can taste His sweetness and feel His breath upon her neck.

We all experience divine kisses. Sometimes they come as a song in the night. Other times they are a Bible verse that leaps off the page and into our soul. Perhaps the kiss comes in the form of a phone call at just the right moment, or as a brush of the Savior's lips as we gaze at a beautiful painting or the splendor of nature.

Jesus's kisses are the expression of His love, His

reassurance He is with us.

When have you experienced a divine kiss?

I've been guilty of brushing divine kisses off as coincidence, or I feel their tingle but rush on without slowing to savor and acknowledge them. It's hard to believe the Creator of the Universe offers that kind of personal attention, so we reason away the very kisses He offers to awaken our hearts to Him.

Even as we start to believe He offers personal attention, we're sometimes afraid. If you're like me, you can find it scary to enter into intimate human relationships, much less one with the Divine. Who knows what deeper relationship with God will bring or require?

Even though I know God is love and has only my best in mind, I've resisted intimacy. Thankfully, the Bridegroom is patient and wise and gentle. When I pull back, the Lord slows down the progression of our relationship to give me time to learn to trust Him. He's good like that. He knows my heart and never ravages it.

He knows your heart, too.

Our sweet Jesus waits until His tender bride realizes her longing for more of Him. "Kiss me again and again!" she cries then. "Your kisses are better than anything else!"

When we cry for intimacy, the Groom can't resist our devotion. He comes running and showers us with kisses. Our hearts open to Him in joy.

Let's pray: Dear Jesus, please help me to know and trust Your love more every day. In Jesus's name I pray. Amen.

Note to Self: You Are Not Alone

By Melissa Henderson

"Seek the Lord and his strength, seek his face
continually."
– 1 Chronicles 16:11 (KJV)

Sunny days bring sounds of laughter and children playing outside. Rainy days bring peaceful sounds of raindrops tapping on the roof. Cloudy days often bring sounds of gentle breezes blowing through the trees, beckoning times of rest. On any of these days, someone may feel alone. A person can feel alone even while surrounded by a crowd of family or friends or strangers.

As we experience the moments of our lives, we often get caught up in day-to-day activities: work, house cleaning, laundry to wash, meals to prepare, bills to pay, errands to run, meetings, church events, afterschool activities, letters and/or emails to read, and a seemingly unending to-do list.

Being busy does not make us fulfilled. There may be a person you know who shows a big smile and a sweet attitude. They appear to have life in order, and all seems to be wonderful. But do we pause and truly visit with that person? Do we pause and share a smile with a stranger?

Do we assume everyone is okay because they don't share their sadness with others? If everything looks fine on the outside, do we just move on with our lives? Are our days filled with rushing here and there, only to fulfill the daily list of tasks?

With many questions to ponder, there are many ways to seek the Lord and His strength. Seek Him always. In the rush of life, seek Him. In the quiet of life, seek Him. When you see a friend or a stranger, offer a smile. Look the person in the eyes and smile. Say hello.

Each one of us has felt alone at times. We are blessed to know we are never truly alone. God is always with us.

During my times of loneliness, depression and anxiety have tried to creep into my thoughts. I am thankful God has given me doctors to help. I am thankful for family, friends, and even strangers who share a smile and say hello.

Reading God's Word (the Holy Bible), sharing time with God, and sharing thoughts with others are reminders I am not alone.

Peace and comfort come over me whenever I seek the Lord, the peace and comfort only He can provide. Trying to solve loneliness or sadness on my own doesn't work for me. Only when I seek Him, the powerful reminder of 1 Chronicles 16:11 shows me that I am never alone.

So even on those days when life is full of activities and time flies by, I will remind myself of His love and comfort. I will remind myself I am not alone.

Let's pray: Lord, my life is so busy at times with errands to do, lists to complete, and places to go. I pray that I will pause and remember that You don't ever rush through Your love for me. You always have time for me. You comfort me and bring peace to me, reminding me I am not alone. Thank You, Father. In Jesus's name I pray. Amen.

Truth in a Troubled World

By Nanci Rubin

"Jesus Christ the same yesterday, and today, and forever."
– Hebrews 13:8 (KJV)

Our world is in such turmoil, and our youth struggle to find their place in an ever-changing environment. Teens look to their peers for acceptance as parental influence becomes almost non-existent. Don't we all look for acceptance? The youth desire to be loved. They need to know God loves them.

I have worked with kids all my life. I was head nurse in the health center at our local university and when I was nursing in the hospital, where I worked in pediatrics. I've taught Sunday school to middle-grade kids. I love children, and I've seen firsthand how easily they can get into trouble.

We're all familiar with the cute toddler who reaches out to grab something, stops, and looks you in the face waiting for your response. A "no-no" will be uttered, and those tiny hands quickly grab the desired object and drop it almost at the same time. They push you beyond your limits. The urge to rebel doesn't seem to go away. Even into adulthood there remains some residual. We appear to like the forbidden thing.

When I worked at the college, some of our freshman students would arrive totally unprepared for the liberal worldview and the freedom associated with being away from home for the first time. It was such a culture shock that some couldn't handle it, and they ended up leaving school. We had a sweet young lady named Rae who was so naïve and easily upset that she refused to sleep in the dorm and received permission from the dean to sleep in the infirmary. She did that her entire freshman year.

It wasn't long into her sophomore year that Rae embraced college life with both arms. I watched her bloom where God planted her. I'm glad we took the time to nurture Rae, as she needed the extra care. She was worth it. However, there is a universal mantra they all relate to. It is, "I hurt, and I'll do anything to stop the pain." And they try to, whether through drugs, promiscuity, or rebellion. They call out for help. But are we listening?

Our young people need validation. They need to know how special they are, not only to their parents, friends, and relatives, but also to God. He created us in His image, so we're starting off ahead in the game of life.

God knows us before we're born. He has chosen us and selected our DNA before we were a glimmer in our mother's eye. I like that. And I'm awed by it. The

Bible says in Jeremiah 1:5 (KJV), "Before I formed thee in the belly I knew thee; and before thou camest forth out of the womb I sanctified thee, and I ordained thee a prophet unto the nations."

I would like every young person, old person, and all in between to realize God didn't make a mistake when He formed you. He made each of us unique and special. No one on Planet Earth has your fingerprint, your thoughts, memories, and your personal quirks. God didn't make junk when He made you!

There is a gentleman in our life group from church who'd seemed troubled for several weeks but never mentioned anything, nor asked for prayer. One evening, he finally asked for prayer. He'd begun to doubt what God had planned for him, and he felt he couldn't be of use to God any longer because of his age. So many seniors believe their age can hinder their work for God. I am reminded that Samson, a Bible character, did greater feats at the end of his life than in the beginning. God is not done with you yet.

No matter your age or station in life, you are God's creation, and He loves you. He has a purpose and a plan for each life. Teach your children in Whom they can believe and count on. God will lead them through life. These are the truths they can hold onto in a troubled world.

Let's pray: Father God, thank You for my family

who taught me about You and the Truth of Your Word. They fed me the Truth until I was able to learn about You myself. Help me to now, in turn, feed others with Your Truth and share Your love with the world. In Jesus's name I pray. Amen.

Perfect Love

By Sara L. Foust

"There is no fear in love; but perfect love casteth out fear: because fear hath torment. He that feareth is not made perfect in love." – 1 John 4:18 (KJV)

Americans spend an astounding amount of money on Valentine's Day-related gifts. Studies show Americans spend more than $20 billion to celebrate this special day. Yet there are all sorts of television episodes that detail the woes of Valentine's Day and the heartache of spending it alone.

I admit I am a fairly simple woman. I'm not a shopper. I don't place a whole lot of value on material possessions because, frankly, my husband and I have never been able to afford a great amount of the "extras." So maybe I am not the best to say Valentine's Day isn't that amazing of a concept. I honestly cannot remember the last time my husband and I celebrated with more than a card or some candy, and that's okay—most of the time.

Sometimes, though, I look at all the extravagant romance and feel a little left out. I see people maybe younger than me discovering blossoming relationships. They dine out frequently and just have that "look"—you know what I'm talking about.

Meanwhile, my life is crazy-busy, and I have five young children depending on me. That doesn't leave much time for romantic dinner dates or even time alone just the two of us (or time alone by myself, for that matter).

Maybe you have the same situation in your life. Maybe you are single and have the innate fear of being alone on Valentine's Day so often portrayed on TV shows. Maybe you are a widow or widower mourning the loss of the love of your life. Or maybe you love Valentine's Day and celebrate with enthusiasm each year with a spouse who is equally enthused.

Yes, Valentine's Day can be an admittedly lonely time of year. But it doesn't have to be. Worldly love is a wonderful thing. The love we have for our spouses, children, parents, friends, and extended family is beautiful. And we, as evidenced by the spending budget for this holiday, pour ourselves into this relational love.

However, it is far from perfect. There are glitches and differences of opinions, hurts, forgotten dates, and sometimes fights. There is a lot of growing required to love another human being, and sometimes, as flawed people, we don't do a very good job of it.

God's love is never like that. His love is the most wonderful, all-encompassing, forgiving, patient, perfect love ever known to the universe. He is incapable of being imperfect. Therefore, the love He showers on us is always perfect in every situation, for every need, and at every moment in life.

When I've felt lonely or sad about the lack of romance in my life, there have been times I've had to remind myself I am covered by the greatest, most powerful love available. I am never alone. I am never forgotten. I am never not loved.

I find that once I focus on that incredible fact, the worries about the lack of romantic moments in my life fizzle away. I am loved by a King! What more could I want?

Let's pray: Dear God, You are so good to me! I am an imperfect sinner who messes up every day, yet You still love me. I don't know how I would face each day without Your perfect love. Thank You for loving me exactly as I am and moving me to become better. In Jesus's name I pray. Amen.

Coming Out of My Cocoon

By Sara L. Foust

"For if we believe that Jesus died and rose again, even so them also which sleep in Jesus will God bring with Him."– 1 Thessalonians 4:14 (KJV)

I absolutely adore Easter. It is by far my favorite holiday. I love everything about it, from the bright colors of new spring outfits to the Easter egg hunts.

Our family gathers each year to eat a big meal and visit. Some of the dads will hide the eggs, while us ladies keep the kids occupied and try to prevent peeking. Then we let them free into the sunshine and listen to their giggles and squeals. After we find all (okay, most) of the eggs, we settle in to open them and see what goodies the kids have found. The children run and play in the (hopefully warm!) yard and enjoy the rest of the day.

We've had a few cold Easters, but I think I tend to block the memories of the chill-out. I'm a lot like a groundhog, I think, or a mama bear. I get into this hunkered-down kind of funk during the winter months, and Easter is the first time I really feel like I'm coming out of my cocoon. It's like I've been asleep all winter, and now I can peel back the layers of gray and stretch into the sunshiny, flowery day of

Easter with a huge smile on my face. With the birds returning and the animals waking, springtime is a wonderful time of rebirth. I don't think it is any mistake on God's part that Easter happens in springtime.

More than anything, though, I adore Easter because of the great love God sent down for us. Without the love of His Son, Jesus, we could never know our own personal reawakening, which is far more than waking up after winter or simply waking up each morning. What Easter represents is the most beautiful love story ever told. Jesus Christ, who was sinless and perfect, chose to take on my sins and bear them to a cross of agony in order to set me free. He died to prove His power over life and death, awakening again on the third day and attaining the victory that can never be taken from Him. And He chose to let me be a part of that eternal reawakening, even though I'm not perfect and even though I don't deserve His mercy and grace.

His birth celebration is important, of course, but without the resurrection, the world never would have seen what a truly miraculous, tradition-breaking, awe-inspiring plan salvation is for humankind. Without Jesus Christ's resurrection, once I slumber in death, that's where I would stay. But because of that mind-bending miracle, the one I can't even try to wrap my humble brain around, I get to go to sleep in death and rise again in Heaven. Doesn't that make you want to shout for joy?

Our Christian holidays have become so commercialized, and generations of children grow up believing trees and eggs and candy and presents are what these holidays are about at their core. I'm so glad I know the truth and am able to teach it to my children. Easter is a great time of reflection on my personal salvation story and a day I can spend in extra prayer thanking Jesus for loving me enough to die for me—and for loving me enough to rise for me and save my soul.

I hope every Easter finds you surrounded by family who loves you, by a church who loves you, and by friends who love you. But I also hope you remember there has never been a more beautiful reason to celebrate. Easter is proof that God loves you enough to want you in Heaven with Him and His Son.

Let's pray: Lord, thank You for Your Son who died for me. I am nothing without Him. Thank You for the blessing of spring and the beauty You surround me with daily. In Jesus's name I pray. Amen.

The Lion and the Lamb

By Sara L. Foust

"And looking upon Jesus as he walked, he saith,
behold the Lamb of God!"
– John 1:36 (KJV)

The arrival of springtime each year makes me so excited. I miss the sun when it is cold and wet all winter. But as soon as it starts to warm up, I am outside soaking in all that glorious Vitamin D from the sunshine.

I love the way the winds blow spring into East Tennessee, as if with each gust it is pulling spring from the other side of the world, bringing it to us in warm breaths.

Wrapped up in the power of those winds, I find myself looking to the Creator, God, and being in awe of His amazing creation. The tiny stems of life that sprout from the ground and in the nests in the trees never cease to amaze me.

Each March I think of the old saying, "In like a lion, out like a lamb." The month of March where I live is often unpredictable. Sometimes warmth creeps in early and sometimes late. Sometimes early warmth fools us into thinking spring is here, then we get slammed with a late snowstorm.

But in the middle of these unpredictable changes, I am reminded of my Savior, whose perfect sacrifice was enough to cleanse me from my sins—not because He changes, but because He changed me. Jesus Christ willingly laid His life down for me, and that truth humbles me because I am not worthy of that kind of sacrifice. There's nothing I could ever do to earn it. Yet He offered Himself as a lamb on a pain-filled cross altar for me. Never had a more perfect sacrifice been found. Never will it be found again.

Jesus Christ protects me with His lion-like majesty and power as He watches over me, guards me, and guides me with each step I take. He protects my soul from harm and lends His power like a blanket over me.

Thank God that Jesus was the perfect sacrificial lamb! Thank God that Jesus loved me enough to suffer and die for me. Praise God that Jesus continues to love me enough to get me through each and every day, to bring me to another beautiful spring every year. I am grateful that He lets me witness the incredible intricacies of His creation daily.

I am grateful for Jesus Christ's two-fold ability to be both the lion and the lamb—to both save and protect, to both humble and make me strong. I am so thankful

God is able to be everything I need.

Aren't you?

Let's pray: What would I do without You, Lord?
You've given me new life, forgiven my sins, and
loved me every day I've breathed. You fiercely
protect me from the enemy, guard my heart against
evil, and stare down the challenges I face with Your
unfailing grace. Thank You. Help me honor You
today, both in my humbleness and my fight to be a
bold testimony of Your love. In Jesus's name I pray.
Amen.

Devotionals about Loving Others

www.capturingtheidea.blogspot.com

One Love

By Jessica Brodie

"For ye are all the children of God by faith in Christ
Jesus. For as many of you as have been baptized into
Christ have put on Christ. There is neither Jew nor
Greek, there is neither bond nor free, there is neither
male nor female: for ye are all one in Christ Jesus."
– Galatians 3:26-28 (KJV)

Ah, the mythology of retail—especially when
Valentine's Day approaches. Stores start rolling out
the hearts, candy, and mushy cards right after
Christmas, and you can't turn on the radio or flip
through a magazine without being bombarded by
jewelry store ads trying to convince us that "nothing
says I love you like diamonds."

February is like one big month of affection and
adoration all wrapped up in dollar signs. You really
can't escape it. Most people I know spend late
January or early February grumbling about so-called
invented holidays or stocking up on dark chocolate
and red and pink décor. Either you roll with it or
resist it.

I've come to look at February—or as I call it, Love
Month—as a time to celebrate all kinds of love, not
just romantic. So while my husband and I do flowers

and sweet trinkets (gotta keep fanning those flames), it's also a golden opportunity for my family to let everyone in our world know how much they mean to us. My kids, along with all their classmates, exchange candy-laden greetings at school. My girlfriends and I swap sweet love-ya-lady messages.

"Love" and "God" are one for me. John the Evangelist defines the very essence of God as love (1 John 4:8). And in that vein, I think it's no coincidence that Black History Month—a time to honor the achievements of African Americans, many whose great works were ignored for centuries simply because of the color of their skin—shares this season. Love means love for all, not just our families and friends. I repeat, all. Sometimes love involves acknowledging the pain of things in the distant or near past. Sometimes it's compassion. Empathy. Kindness.

Jesus gave us two commandments that take precedence over everything: to love God with every ounce of our being, and to love others as ourselves (Matthew 22:36-40). We've known this for 2,000 years now. Why, then, are our cities and communities still rife with racial tension and hate?

If we strive to be Christian, that means we are committing ourselves to be Jesus-followers. And we cannot follow the Christ without following His commands. "Love others" doesn't just mean love your spouse or your inner circle, or love people who look or sound just like you. "Love others" means stepping outside our comfortable societal-imposed boundaries to view the world through a God lens: the understanding that in Christ we are all children of God.

One of my favorite verses is from the Apostle Paul's letter to the Galatians: "For ye are all the children of God by faith in Christ Jesus. For as many of you as have been baptized into Christ have put on Christ. There is neither Jew nor Greek, there is neither bond nor free, there is neither male nor female: for ye are all one in Christ Jesus." (Galatians 3:26-28 KJV)

We're in this together.

It doesn't matter what we look like on the outside, what color our skin is, or what language we speak. It doesn't matter if we're young or old or male or female. One means one. One body, one Spirit, one God—all of us wrapped up together.

I encourage you to push yourself beyond the boundaries of what we'd traditionally call "love" and heed our call to love all people as God loves us: with benevolence, concern, and goodwill. Love the homeless person on the corner. Love the snotty salesclerk. Love the driver who cuts you off in traffic. Put yourself in their shoes. See the world in their eyes. Try to feel their pain and their frustration for a moment, and watch how it changes you.

Maybe nothing says, "I love you" like diamonds for some. But for me, I'd much rather say I love you in more meaningful ways: by truly seeing another person, by cultivating a generous and empathetic heart, by seeking God first in my thoughts and actions toward others, and by cultivating kindness and compassion.

One love, one God, now and forever.

My Prayer: Heavenly Father, society tells us the best gifts are things, especially things that cost money. But as Your children, we know these things are earthly and temporary. Help us to love others with gifts that are eternal: kindness and empathy, prayer and good counsel, compassion and a listening ear. In Jesus's name I pray. Amen.

Overcoming Stress through Love and Service

By Jessica Brodie

"If there be therefore any consolation in Christ, if any comfort of love, if any fellowship of the Spirit, if any bowels and mercies, Fulfil ye my joy, that ye be likeminded, having the same love, being of one accord, of one mind.
Let nothing be done through strife or vainglory; but in lowliness of mind let each esteem other better than themselves. Look not every man on his own things, but every man also on the things of others."
– Philippians 2:1-4 (KJV)

I've been a giant ball of tension and stress recently: kids, work, illness, and a silly-but-debilitating fitness-inspired injury—you name it.

Even though I've been trying hard to breathe, to rest in the presence of my Creator, and give all my concerns to the Lord, the fact remains that I'm doing too much, not giving myself enough downtime, running on empty, and not getting quite enough shuteye. And it's been taking a toll.

As I write this, I'm also knee-deep in preparations to head off with my husband on a one-week mission trip to help hurricane victims in Puerto Rico. And ironically, I know deep down the trip, more than anything else I could possibly do, is my ticket to stress-busting.

I know it's not going to be easy. We'll be staying in the mountains in rather rustic conditions with no electricity, and the work will be grueling: tarping, tear-out, roofing, rebuild. But if I've gleaned one bit of wisdom in my life so far, it's that pushing myself aside to focus on others is probably the best stress-reliever in existence.

We all know Jesus said the two greatest commandments are, first, to love God with everything we are, and second, to love our neighbors as ourselves (Matthew 22:35-40).

But what we might not know is that the secret to bliss also has everything to do with keeping those commandments. In today's me-driven secular society, we get so many mixed messages about happiness. We're told we need to prioritize ourselves and do what feels right. But as Christians, we need to ignore that and instead focus on turning ourselves over to the Lord in whatever way He calls us to do. Sacrificing—our time, our money, our material possessions, our very lives—helps us become one with God.

Why do we think Jesus taught that it is more blessed to give than receive? I think He was saying worry over ourselves and our needs is a consuming, ever-downward-spiraling track to despair. His path is the one we are to follow: the way of truth, love, and humble service with God at the center.

The Apostle Paul wrote in his letter to the Philippians, "If there be therefore any consolation in Christ, if any comfort of love, if any fellowship of the Spirit, if any bowels and mercies, Fulfil ye my joy, that ye be likeminded, having the same love, being of one accord, of one mind. Let nothing be done through strife or vainglory; but in lowliness of mind let each esteem other better than themselves. Look not every man on his own things, but every man also on the things of others." (Philippians 2:1-4, KJV).

Loving others, for me, is serving others. Whether that service is through reading to kids, cooking a meal for people in need, being a shoulder for a friend (or stranger), being an encourager, or hopping on a plane for a weeklong mission trip to Puerto Rico, you can be sure of one thing: Putting myself on the backburner to engage in some love-filled Christian service is a healing balm to the soul.

Let's pray: Father God, I can be my own worst enemy at times. But I know the solution is not focusing inward but instead outward: on You, on others, on doing good works in Your name. When I am overwhelmed with stress, help me look beyond myself to see how I can be Your hands and feet in the world around me. In Jesus's name I pray. Amen.

Gracious Words

By Melissa Henderson

"Pleasant words are as an honeycomb, sweet to the
soul, and health to the bones."
– Proverbs 16:24 (KJV)

Have you considered your words lately? What about
your thoughts? Who did you have conversations with
today? Reflecting back on this day and recent times,
have you shown the glory of God in your words and
actions?

Each day, we are given opportunities to shine God's
love to others. When things are going great and life is
lovely, we are happy to share good news and be
joyful in discussions with others.

But what about those times when life is tough and we
feel like venting? Those times when someone cuts in
front of us in the traffic line, someone gives a not-so-
nice opinion, or something happens at your job and
you feel like you could scream. How do you handle
those times? Are your words soothing and calming,
gracious and sweet to the soul? Or are your words
angry and defensive, bitter to you and to others?

These are times when we definitely need to pause and
ask God for help. Ask Him for peace of mind and

heart. Ask Him for the words He would like you to share with others. God knows our hearts, and He knows exactly what we need.

Imagine having a conversation with someone and the words from the other person are hurtful and angry. Maybe tears flow as your first reaction was disbelief at what was being said. Your next reaction might be to defend yourself, or go on the offense with hurtful words. How would that help the situation?

Instead, what if you walked away from the conversation? What about pausing to pray and asking God for the words He wants you to share? Or maybe God wants you to stay quiet in this particular instance. Ask Him for guidance.

How do you feel when someone gives you a compliment? When words spoken to you are gracious and sweet to the soul? Does that kindness cause you to want to respond in kindness?

Do you easily lift up others with gracious words and friendliness? We may never know what someone is experiencing in their life. Gracious words can change the perspective of a person who needs love and kindness.

Say hello to the cashier at the store, to the letter carrier, to a neighbor. Ask "How are you?" then truly pause to listen to the answer. Visit a nursing home and listen to the stories of the people there. Their lives are full of magnificent journeys. Take a walk in the neighborhood on the weekend; it often brings a chance to speak with people we may not see during the week.

Listen to how you speak to others, in person and on the phone. Are you shining God's love in your words and your actions? A smile along with friendly words can soothe and heal the heart.

Listen to the way people speak to you. Is there something bothering them and they need comfort by your words?

Words are a very special way to show others His love and grace. I pray that today will be a day full of gracious words.

Let's pray: Dear God, words can lift our moods or cause us to be sad. Thank You for giving us words to comfort and share compassion. I pray that I will remember to use words wisely and to pray before I speak. In Jesus's name I pray. Amen.

Fighting Fair

By Jessica Brodie

"Put on therefore, as the elect of God, holy and beloved, bowels of mercies, kindness, humbleness of mind, meekness, longsuffering; Forbearing one another, and forgiving one another, if any man have a quarrel against any: even as Christ forgave you, so also do ye. And above all these things put on charity, which is the bond of perfectness."
– Colossians 3:12-14 (KJV)

One of the hardest things I've learned to do in my marriage is fight fairly, but it's been the most critical love lesson of all. For when it's done right, I've learned, God is at the core.

See, at the heart of how a couple argues is how they relate to each other, how they respect each other. In the best scenarios, arguing stems from care, from a place of love, typically from frustration about a small or large issue threatening the peace of the home in some way. You might be bickering about how big of a house to purchase or some perceived slight, or it might be deeper, like a dark secret now come to light.

Healthy, loving marriages—just like healthy, loving friendships—don't avoid issues, sweeping them out the door and hoping they'll fly away. They shine holy light into the darkness, and in that light, a deeper love emerges.

Throughout the New Testament, early Christians are called to hold each other accountable. The Apostle Paul frequently acknowledges that disagreements happen. People sin, whether intentionally or not. But as he instructs the nascent church, don't ignore the problem. Address it. As he says in Galatians 6:1 (KJV), "Brethren, if a man be overtaken in a fault, ye which are spiritual, restore such an one in the spirit of meekness; considering thyself, lest thou also be tempted," or in Ephesians 4:25 (KJV), "Wherefore putting away lying, speak every man truth with his neighbour: for we are members one of another."

Be honest, he's saying. If the argument has to do with a sin on someone's part, gently tell the one you love there's a problem, and urge him or her toward repentance.

Gently. That's the key word here. I'm not saying you should have scrappy yelling matches or those long periods of the silent treatment. That's just reacting, not communicating. When we address an issue in a God-oriented manner, we are to do it with love and consideration, not accusation and anger.

Paul ends Ephesians 4:32 (KJV) saying, "And be ye kind one to another, tenderhearted, forgiving one another, even as God for Christ's sake hath forgiven you."

Those same sentiments are reflected in his advice to the Colossians: "Put on therefore, as the elect of God, holy and beloved, bowels of mercies, kindness, humbleness of mind, meekness, longsuffering;
Forbearing one another, and forgiving one another, if any man have a quarrel against any: even as Christ forgave you, so also do ye. And above all these things put on charity, which is the bond of perfectness." (Colossians 3:12-14, KJV).

Of course, not all arguments are that simple. Maybe you think your spouse or friend has sinned against you, but the proverbial log in your eye is preventing you from seeing your own sin in the situation. Or maybe you're being called out for misunderstood or unintentional behavior and you feel hurt that your loved one would judge your actions in this way. Maybe one of you is just plain grumpy.

The best and only way through it is that one "greatest" attribute: Love.

Happily, Paul defines "love" also known as "charity" for us too, in 1 Corinthians 13:4-7 (KJV): "Charity suffereth long, and is kind; charity envieth not; charity vaunteth not itself, is not puffed up, Doth not behave itself unseemly, seeketh not her own, is not easily provoked, thinketh no evil; Rejoiceth not in iniquity, but rejoiceth in the truth; Beareth all things, believeth all things, hopeth all things, endureth all things."

God is love. He commands us to love others as ourselves, to show our faith through our love, to point to Him through our love.

So when it comes to arguments, remember: The only way to win is for everyone to win. If you come through a battle with one arm unscathed but the other broken and bloody, you're still injured.

We are one body, literally and figuratively.

Let's pray: Heavenly Father, sometimes when we fight we see the world through one set of eyes: our own. Help us to see we are part of a unit—one body in You. In Jesus's name I pray. Amen.

Showing God's Love

By Melissa Henderson

"And the people asked him, saying, What shall we do
then? He answereth and saith unto them, He that hath
two coats, let him impart to him that hath none; and
he that hath meat, let him do likewise."
– Luke 3:10-11 (KJV)

Today was a typical warm, humid and breezy day in
coastal South Carolina. The bright rays of sunshine
burst forth from the puffy clouds in between rain
sprinkles. At one moment, the sky looked as if rain
would moisten the ground all day. The next moment,
sunshine seemed to be positioned in the sky and not
ready to leave.

A black pickup truck filled with construction supplies
arrived and parked in front of our neighbor's house.
The same pickup truck had been coming and going
all week. Several men would step out of the vehicle
each morning and begin carrying tools and supplies
to the back yard. Our neighbor was having a patio
installed at the back of her house, and the same
gentlemen showed up each day and began the task at
hand.

One day, that project was completed, and a new
project began. Those hard workers not only installed

patios, but they could also power wash homes and driveways. My husband and I watched from the inside of our air-conditioned home, fascinated by their work and dedication to the tasks. These guys worked hard. We didn't know their names, but we watched to make sure they were okay in the heat. One man was older, and there were several younger men.

This afternoon, I noticed the black truck was gone, and two men were sitting on a ladder. They seemed to be waiting for a ride. Their work was finished for the day, and their bodies looked exhausted. Sweaty shirts, sweat on their brows, and slow movements showed how the work had tired them.

A thought crossed my mind. "Wonder if they are thirsty? Wonder if we should take them some water?" As quickly as the thoughts entered my mind, I became distracted with something else. I had seen an opportunity to show God's love and I had let it slip by, distracted by a meaningless thought about something else.

Shortly afterward, I heard voices outside. Still, I waited and completed what I was doing instead of checking on the gentlemen.

As I walked downstairs, my husband was coming in the front door. "I took some water to the guys out front. They are waiting for their ride. I asked them if they would like some water and they said, 'Yes' and 'thank you.'"

I am very proud of my husband. He saw a possible need, and he acted on his nudge from God. I did not act, thinking I would do something later. I am upset with myself, but I am thankful my husband opened his heart and offered kindness to strangers.

Too often, we postpone acts of kindness, thinking we will do something later. But now is the time to show God's love. Don't put off a nudge from God. Someone might have a need you can help with, and you are given that opportunity by God to show compassion and kindness.

Can you think of times when you wanted to show kindness and put off the chance, thinking you could do something later? When God used my husband to express His love by giving a bottle of water to some strangers, they had been shown the love of God.

We may never see these gentlemen again. But I will remember them, even though I never learned their names or anything about them. They gave me a lesson today, and I will remember that lesson.

God's love can be shown in many ways. How are you showing His love to others?

Let's pray: Father God, please open my eyes and

heart to notice the needs of others. Give me the desire to share Your love and care. I thank You for all the blessings You provide. In Jesus's name I pray. Amen.

Lessons on How to Love

By Jessica Brodie

"But when Jesus saw it, he was much displeased, and said unto them, Suffer the little children to come unto me, and forbid them not: for of such is the kingdom of God. Verily I say unto you, Whosoever shall not receive the kingdom of God as a little child, he shall not enter therein."– Mark 10:14-15 (KJV)

I don't know if you'd classify me as an introvert or a highly sensitive person, but as much as I love people, I get overwhelmed after most encounters. Whether it's a meeting or a one-on-one with a friend, I have to decompress in the car after—or if it's a biggie, come home and take a nap. (And I despise naps.)

But it just so happens I'm a member of one of the largest United Methodist churches in the nation, which also just so happens to offer a massive vacation Bible school. Its VBS attracts about 2,000 children and hundreds of volunteers who descend on the campus all week long.

When the leaders put out their plea for help, the Holy Spirit began to stir in me. Me! An introverted, overly sensitive soul! Immediately, I knew what I needed to do: sign up to love on those kids. And no, not as a behind-the-scenes helper or an at-home prayer warrior or anything else … but as a crew guide for fourth and fifth-grade girls and boys.

Right smack in the middle of all the action.

I knew full well what it meant: All week long I'd be in the thick of the noise and interaction, the dancing and songs, the water games and scavenger hunts.

But I couldn't help myself. The Spirit had called, and I needed to answer. What else could I do but throw myself in, give it all I had, and face the consequences later?

I'm glad I did. It was spectacular!

My husband thought I was wacko. Every afternoon after VBS I was a wreck, and by Friday I'm not sure I even bothered to brush my hair, but oh—what an experience! On Monday, we were spelling out "Jesus" on the floor with our bodies. On Tuesday, I got soaked head-to-toe from a water bucket race. By Wednesday, I'd mastered all the dance moves to the praise songs. On Thursday, I watched as kids went to the altar and accepted Jesus as their savior. On Friday, I sat back dazed, and recognized the week for what it was: a holy masterpiece. Before my eyes, preteen boys were singing their hearts out. Girls were shrieking, faces streaked with pure, undiluted, Disney World-level glee.

It was a God Party, and I'd just gotten a weeklong front row view.

It hit me then—that's what Jesus meant when He told His disciples, "But when Jesus saw it, he was much displeased, and said unto them, Suffer the little children to come unto me, and forbid them not: for of such is the kingdom of God. Verily I say unto you, Whosoever shall not receive the kingdom of God as a little child, he shall not enter therein." (Mark 10:14-15, KJV).

These kids were wide open. They came to VBS as themselves, quirks and bad habits and crazy hair and shining eyes. They took in what was taught. They reveled in it, and they left exhilarated and energized. The way they received the Kingdom of God—with passion and authenticity, holding nothing back—was a holy example of how God wants us to love Him and how we should love each other.

These kids taught me far more than I taught them. I'm ashamed now of my early reluctance to volunteer just because I was afraid of a little discomfort. Watching those kids taught me how to love in a fresh, new way—with arms wide open, voice raised, hair wild, caught up in the only thing that really matters: worshipping our Lord.

Next year, I won't let my reluctance hinder me from loving those kids the way Jesus demanded. You can bet I'll be right there in the action, dancing and singing and laughing.

And then going home and taking a nap.

Let's pray: God, I know that one of the best things I can do for You is help bring others into Your Kingdom. Help me to push aside my own discomfort and do what I can to help guide the "little ones" to You. Help awaken in me a heart to serve You despite my own hesitations. In Jesus's name I pray. Amen.

Hopefully Devoted

By Jessica Brodie

"Be kindly affectioned one to another with brotherly
love; in honour preferring one another."
– Romans 12:10 (KJV)

When I think of the word "devoted," my Gram
immediately comes to mind.

A child of The Great Depression, she learned to make
do in a tough world. She moved with her entire
family to Miami from Brooklyn, New York, when
she was thirteen, and by the time she came of age,
World War II was in full swing. She met and married
her husband, my grandfather, at age nineteen, and
raised three kids in the suburbs while working as a
bookkeeper and keeping house.

I loved him dearly, but I imagine my Gramps wasn't
an easy man to be married to. Yet my Gram was
always there by his side, completely devoted to him
in spite of his temper and other quirks best left to
time.

When her children grew up and left home, Gram
continued to be a devoted wife, but also a woman
devoted to many others in her life. Her widowed
mom began a battle with Alzheimer's, and so my

great-grandmother moved in with them, and Gram became her full-time caregiver until my great-grandmother's death. Shortly after her passing, my Great-Aunt Ethel took ill. Again, Gram didn't hesitate—Aunt Ethel moved right into the vacant spare bedroom, and there she remained, happy and well-loved until her death.

Over the years, Gram took in a host of people in need—my cousin Vikki and Vikki's young son when they fell on hard times, her childhood friend Annie when Annie's family no longer had enough space, and eventually my Gramps himself between his cancer and a long and difficult battle with dementia. Even a litter of alley-kittens (in spite of Gram's horrible cat allergy!) became her "flock."

In her care and devotion for others, Gram embodied love. She embodied Jesus.

Gram's love and devotion brings to mind for me the Apostle Paul's reminder to the early church to "Be kindly affectioned one to another with brotherly love; in honour preferring one another." (Romans 12:10, KJV).

Devotion is a big word. Essentially, it means "all-in." It's a sacrifice of self, a sacrifice much like Jesus made for us on the cross: one that sometimes saps our strength and our pocketbooks, our time and our energy. It means giving relentlessly, radically, fully.

It's the kind of love embodied by my Gram, who gave of her body, her soul, her time, her heart, her home, her finances—everything she had to care for those under her watch.

Be devoted, as God is, was, and has always been to us—a nonstop, all-in, all-consuming, total love. For in loving others, we love God. And we model God's love for us.

I pray I can follow in my Gram's footsteps in my devotion to those in my world—family, friends, neighbors, and those in need.

Let's pray: Dear God, some days I know I get so caught up in myself that I focus only on my own needs. But You call me to love others as much as I love myself. Help me to look beyond my own circumstances to show kindness, assistance, and compassion to people around me. Help me see I can show my love for You by loving others well. In Jesus's name I pray. Amen.

Alexis A. Goring

Devotionals about Turning to Others for Help

www.capturingtheidea.blogspot.com

What Do You Have in Your House?

By Quantrilla Ard

"And Elisha said unto her, What shall I do for thee?
Tell me what has thou in the house? And she said,
Thine handmaid hath not any thing in the house, save
a pot of oil." – 2 Kings 4:2 (KJV)

A few years back, I was searching for something. I couldn't quite put my finger on it, but it kept me up at night, concerned me throughout the day, and quite honestly, had me in an overall sour mood. I tried to put a brave face on and cover up this discontentment through being busy. I was a wife, mom, student, and church secretary at the time, so there was no shortage of tasks from which to choose. But there was a void of sorts.

In trying to figure out my feelings, I came across a passage of Scripture that changed the direction of my life forever.

It wasn't that I didn't know the story. I'm sure I had heard it before growing up. Yet this time, something clicked and came alive in my heart. It literally moved me to tears. In Chapter 2 of the Bible book of 2 Kings, Elisha had just received the double portion of God's spirit after Elijah was translated and he begins to do miracles. Two chapters later, we find a certain woman in a precarious situation, a woman who happened to be a widow of one of the sons of the prophets—the same group of men who'd trained under Elijah.

The Bible says she cried to Elisha because the creditor had come to take her two sons to be servants in order to pay off the debt they had no doubt accumulated since the passing of her husband. Elisha asked her, "What shall I do for you?" Then he follows up with another question, "What do you have in your house?"

Now, this was interesting! I'm sure this woman had probably sold any and everything of value to pay what they owed. She replied that there was nothing, "Save a pot of oil" (2 Kings 4:2).

Next, Elisha told her to do something that stretched her way out of her comfort zone. It wasn't that she lacked faith; she knew Elisha, through the power of God, could help her. So what did she lack? I'm not sure. But what I know for sure is this to be true: When you are down and in the depths of despair, you do not feel like going to anyone asking for anything. At all. And here it is that her salvation was dependent on her ability to set her pride aside and ask for help from people she had probably tried to hide her situation from the whole time. Mercy!

Elisha told her to borrow empty vessels from all her neighbors, and not just a few. Can you imagine the stares and looks of confusion? Then, she was to come back home, shut herself and her sons in, and pour that leftover oil into all the vessels, setting the full ones to the side. While pouring out, she asked one of her sons to bring her another vessel, and he replied that there was not one left to fill. The oil remained. Hallelujah, the oil remained!

She tells Elisha what she had done, and he responds with one last task. According to 2 Kings 4:7 (KJV), he says, "Go, sell the oil, and pay thy debt, and live thou and thy children off the rest." The end.

When I think about this story and the pain and fear that were such large parts of it, I am brought to tears. Like the widow, I have often found myself in situations in which I am literally empty—situations in which I have sold everything in my "house" and cannot identify anything left of merit or value. I cry out to God asking Him to fix my destitute mess, and He asks me, "Beloved, what's in your house?"

This question urges me to look for my pot of oil, that thing I've overlooked because I've not assigned it much worth. God then instructs me to go to my neighbors, to tell my story, to ask them for vessels to pour my oil in. "What miracle can come from that?" you may ask. Dear friend, I'll tell you. Full vessels of oil—plenty, supply, met need, overflow, and freedom from the surety of bondage! Thank You, Jesus.

So did I ever find what it was I was searching for? Absolutely! God revealed to me through His Word, the Holy Bible, that what I needed was already in my purview. I didn't need to look elsewhere to fill the void I was experiencing, I simply needed to take inventory of my house and find my oil.

I guess all that's left to ask is, "What's in your house?"

Let's pray: Lord, I thank You that all I need is in You. Help me to remember how You've provided in the past, and that all I need to do is ask You to provide again. Please show me how to put aside my fear in asking for help because of my limited perspective. You have a thousand ways to bless me. Show me how to rejoice in whichever way You choose. In Jesus's name I pray. Amen.

The Heart of Hospitality

By Melissa Henderson

"Distributing to the necessity of saints; given to
hospitality."
– Romans 12:13 (KJV)

How can I serve others and show God's love?

Pause for a moment and think of people around you,
both people you know and people who are strangers.
How would you respond if they needed something?
A meal, a ride to the doctor, or a ride to the grocery
store? What if all they needed was a simple hello or a
visit?

Needs come in all sizes. From major needs to minor
needs, at one time or another, we all need someone.
There are times when we feel comfortable asking for
help, and other times, we decide not to ask for help.
Maybe it's the feeling we're being a bother, or we
think maybe someone else needs more help than we
do. So we don't ask. We try to accomplish things on
our own or just give up in despair. Maybe we are
embarrassed to need assistance.

I have experienced vertigo for more than twenty-five
years. Never knowing when a dizzy spell will occur
can be very scary. There is a difference between

dizziness and vertigo, and it is very hard to explain to someone who has not experienced one or the other.

When I was first diagnosed with vertigo, I decided to stop driving as I didn't want to put others or myself in danger. Some people could not understand my inability to drive. I look perfectly fine on the outside, with no outward signs of any illness or medical condition. Yet my body would not allow me to enjoy activities of the past.

Not being able to drive caused me to miss volunteer meetings and special events. My husband works full time, and taking time off from work every time I needed to go somewhere was not an option. He is very understanding about my condition and realizes some days are better than others for me.

Then came my decision to ask others for help. Not wanting to be a burden caused me to postpone asking for help in the beginning. People have their own lives and schedules. Who would want to disrupt their life to drive me to appointments? Would anyone have the extra time?

Praying and asking God what to do in this situation was vital. He answered my prayers. Once I gave my worries to God, a sense of relief filled my heart and soul. I began sharing my story. As I shared, friends and strangers told me about their conditions and knowledge of vertigo. Friends learned of my vertigo and began offering rides to my appointments and activities. I only needed to ask, and my request was answered. There was no need for me to be embarrassed or feel like a burden.

What a blessing! Keeping quiet had caused me more worry. Sharing and asking for help brought peace and comfort.

Some friends even shared that they were blessed through being a blessing to me. We never know when we may need to lean on others for help. God has given us blessings in those who practice hospitality.

Have you helped someone lately? Have you been a blessing? I encourage you to pause and think of ways you can be a blessing to someone. Simple ways like smiles, waving hello, a phone call, a note in the mail, and yes, offering a ride to someone who can't drive are all ways to show God's love.

Let's pray: Father God, thank You for providing ways for us to help others. Thank You for the people You have sent to give me peace and comfort during times of uncertainty. May I always be ready to help others. In Jesus's name I pray. Amen.

Helping Others is Loving Others

By Jessica Brodie

"My little children, let us not love in word, neither in
tongue; but in deed and in truth."
– 1 John 3:18 (KJV)

I'm not sure when or why I started having trouble
accepting help from others.

Constructive criticism is fine, and words of wisdom
are always welcome. But accepting actual physical
help—whether that's someone teaching me to use a
weed-eater or taking my kids for the day so I can
write—is difficult for me. I fear that I'm taking
advantage of my friends, or I'm being a "mooch" or a
"taker." I get flashbacks of a mine-mine-mine
childhood when I'd hoard my lunch or my toys, and I
fear I'll backslide into that slippery slope of
selfishness.

If I'm being brutally honest, I think deep down, I'm
also worried I'll be indebted to someone else. And
yet I love to help others—not because it makes me
feel like big-shot "Jessica to the Rescue" either, but
because it feels good to let my servant's heart soar
and do stuff for people. I offer to host playdates and
bring my friends' kids to and from places frequently.
I don't ever feel like they're less than me, nor do I

feel they owe me something or that they're taking advantage of me.

So why, when it's my turn to be on the receiving end, do I feel so uncomfortable about it? The other day, I had a full slate of activities and appointments lined up, including a summer camp and two performances for one of my kids, but my husband's car unexpectedly needed service and he needed to borrow mine to drive to the other side of the state for a meeting.

I texted a few pals, and all of a sudden I had friends to the rescue! One friend brought my daughter to kids' worship music camp so I could work from home. Three hours later at lunchtime, another friend drove all the way across town to pick me up so I could see my daughter's camp finale performance, then dropped me back off at home and took her on to their house for a swimming playdate, then brought her home hours later. A third friend brought her to the theater that evening, and when my husband finally got home, I hopped in the car to go watch her perform.

At first, it didn't seem so bad to be carless and relying on friends to get everything done, but by the time the evening rolled around, I felt like a colossal scrounger. I kept apologizing and thanking people all over the place, not to mention furiously calculating exactly how and when I could reciprocate their kindness.

Finally, one of my friends gave me a patient smile and said, "Girl, please. Friends do this stuff for each other. It's really no sweat."

She's right. John the Evangelist writes in his first epistle that we should "not love in word, neither in tongue; but in deed and in truth." (1 John 3:18 KJV). Helping others, caring for others, feeding others—anything we physically do for others is a way to show love for others, and love is something Jesus specifically calls us to do. In fact, we're not just to show this extravagant love for friends but for all—strangers and enemies included.

Accepting help from my friends is allowing them to be obedient to God by showing love for me, and that's always a good thing.

Let's Pray: Heavenly Father, help me understand that accepting help from others is not weakness. Their help is a love offering they are trying to show me in Your name. Help me not be a hindrance to that. In Jesus's name I pray. Amen.

What a Friend We Have in Jesus

By Melissa Henderson

"For the mountains shall depart, and the hills be removed; but my kindness shall not depart from thee, neither shall the covenant of my peace be removed, saith the Lord that hath mercy on thee."
– Isaiah 54:10 (KJV)

Living near ponds and rivers means there are new and different creatures to learn about. From alligators to lizards to snakes, I am learning more than I ever wanted to know about these creatures.

Recently, I looked out my side window and noticed a snake sunning itself on my neighbor's front doormat. Since I am afraid of snakes and my husband was at work, I called my next-door neighbor on the other side of the house. This man enjoys all kinds of wildlife, and whenever I see something that scares me or causes me concern, this nice neighbor comes to the rescue.

The neighbor, his wife, and one of their grandchildren came right over to calm me. The lady in the house where the snake was sunning came to the front window and looked at us standing in the yard. We motioned to her that we were watching something.

Going through her back door, she gathered with us. I was afraid. I prayed for the snake to go away. It did—but traveling into the siding of the house next door was not where we had intended that thing to end up.

My neighbors, who are interested in nature, truly comforted me. The nice man and his granddaughter taught me some things about nature.

After several attempts to find the creature, everyone went home. Each time the friends returned home, the snake returned outside to sun. Each time I saw it, I called the neighbor again. Yet my neighbors were patient and kind. They never complained about me calling them because I was scared. Each time, they came to my yard and chatted with me.

After numerous calls to the neighbors, I finally spotted the snake slithering back to the creek behind the neighborhood. I hope it doesn't come back any time soon.

Through all this stressful time, I thanked God for neighbors who comfort and come whenever I call. They are busy with their own activities. They could have just told me not to worry and went on about their daily routines. Yet each time, the neighbors came to my house, comforted me and made me feel safe.

Through this whole situation, friends comforted me, but most of all, God comforted me. He assured me of His unfailing love and compassion. His peace will not be removed.

Let's pray: Thank You, Lord, for friends and strangers who come to give help when we call. You have placed those people in our lives for a reason. What a blessing to be able to call for help and know that You will provide. In Jesus's name I pray. Amen.

Alexis A. Goring

Devotionals about Hope and Miracles

Devotionals for the Heart

www.capturingtheidea.blogspot.com

Someone's Rooting for Us

By Gail Kittleson

"And as they thus spake, Jesus himself stood in the midst of them, and saith unto them, Peace be unto you. But they were terrified and affrighted, and supposed that they had seen a spirit. And he said unto them, Why are ye troubled? and why do thoughts arise in your hearts? Behold my hands and my feet, that it is I myself: handle me, and see; for a spirit hath not flesh and bones, as ye see me have. And when he had thus spoken, he shewed them his hands and his feet. And while they yet believed not for joy, and wondered, he said unto them, Have ye here any meat?"
– Luke 24:36-41 (KJV)

It's impossible to center on just one verse today because we need the context in order to understand the monumental event in history that's going on. What we see in this passage is the aftermath of Jesus's suffering and death. We see resurrection. Along with that picture, God reveals His desire for us to believe.

If you've ever tried to convince a child to try some new delight, but they first have to overcome their fear, you recognize the emotional set-up of this scene. It's like teaching a child the joys of bicycle riding. They've learned a lot on their tricycle, but there's so much more ahead ... if only they can believe and plunge into this new arena.

The disciples had gotten to know Jesus on earth, but they'd also seen Him die on the cross. Now, He must convince them that, against all odds, He's still—or newly—alive. Of course, this makes no sense to them, even though He prepared them in many ways for His resurrection.

We note in the passage how Jesus opened Himself up. He said, "Look .... Touch ... Look me over." He made himself fully available to His disciples. Then He appealed to their logical-mindedness: "A ghost doesn't have muscle and bone like this."

What conclusion does that thought lead to? This is not a ghost. He ties this experience to another one in His history with these men—once before, they thought He was a ghost when He came to them walking on the water. If not a ghost, then this must be Jesus!

A little later, He asked if they had any food and munched some leftover fish right then and there. It's as if He couldn't do enough to help them believe.

When I think of all the times I've tried so hard to believe, but still doubted, I was failing to see Jesus in this way, as our instructor and cheerleader. He knows it's tough for His friends to embrace what's happened, but He's determined. We can come to believe little by little.

As we face our trials, He's on our side, like a watchful parent or another kind adult. He assesses every angle of each situation, guiding us to the kind of help we need. He's not our enemy in the struggle for our faith. He's our truest Friend.

Let's pray: Help us, Lord, to realize You're rooting for us and willing to do whatever it takes to help us learn. In Jesus's name I pray. Amen.

Twinkle Light Promise

By Paula Moldenhauer

"Ye are the light of the world. A city that is set on an hill cannot be hid. Neither do men light a candle, and put it under a bushel, but on a candlestick; and it giveth light unto all that are in the house. Let your light so shine before men, that they may see your good works, and glorify your Father which is in heaven."
– Matthew 5:14-16 (KJV)

Our first Christmas tree had only white lights. For years, held in bondage to a legalist understanding of Christmas, we'd skipped the Christmas tree, but I was hungry to express joy at the thought of Christ's birth, so I hung white lights in the window as a reminder that Jesus, the Light of the World, came to save us from darkness within and without. All other decorations in the years to come built upon that first strand of lights, just as our lives begin with and build on Jesus.

Life is illuminated by Jesus's grace and truth. Our thoughts, identity, and decisions are illuminated by His light.

Where there is light, darkness flees. It doesn't matter how the enemy lied to us or who tried to steal light from us. It doesn't matter because Jesus, the Light of the World, is with us now. Darkness cannot exist in the presence of light.

Jesus chases the darkness away. His light heals us. His light leads us to freedom.

Jesus is the Word incarnate. The Word is a lamp to our feet, a light to our path.

Jesus, our Light, reveals next steps—steps of life-giving light.

In Jesus is life, and His life is the light of all mankind. The darkness of this world has not overcome His light. It cannot! (John 1:4)

God's light is pure. In Him there is no darkness at all (1 John 1:5).

He not only lights our way, He lights us! We are like the Christmas tree. It can sit unnoticed, deep in a forest. When night comes, it is shrouded in darkness. But when wrapped in twinkle lights, that same tree cannot be hidden.

When we are illuminated by the Light of Jesus Christ, we light up our space in this world. We are like Him: pure, white light, like a city set on a hill that can't be hidden. It's like a lamp or a candle set in the middle of a dark room.

Even in the dark times of our lives or of the world, His light shines in us and through us.

In this world of suicide bombers, gunmen in schools, and war in the Middle East, the darkness fights for position. In this world of hidden abuses that tear at personal worth and identity, darkness tries to suffocate.

But it cannot win.

In the most inky, black darkness, the tiniest light always pushes back the black. Whole caverns of darkness cannot overcome one little flickering candle.

There is no greater worship than a life surrendered to the Light. Surrendered lives pierce the darkness as they lift glowing arms to point to Jesus, the Light of the world.

Let's pray: Jesus, You are perfect light. In You there is no darkness at all. I surrender to Your light. Take it deep inside me and heal me. Shine it at my feet and guide my next steps. Glow within me, lighting me up from the inside out that I may bring glory to Your name. In Jesus's name I pray. Amen.

What Is His Name?

By Quantrilla Ard

"For unto us a child is born, unto us a son is given:
and the government shall be upon his shoulder: and
his name shall be called Wonderful, Counsellor, The
mighty God, The everlasting Father, The Prince of
Peace."
– Isaiah 9:6 (KJV)

I remember having grand ideas of what my children's
names would be when I became a parent. I would
spend hours searching through websites and books,
trying to put together the right combination of first
and middle names, although I wasn't sure of what
their last names would be (this began long before I
was married). The sound of the name was important
as I waded through names both traditional and non-
traditional, and it had to have just the right ring to it.
What I didn't always take into account was the
meaning of the names, and I am glad that I had a few
more years yet to ultimately make that decision.

A saying that I hear quite often in my writing and
professional circles is "Words mean things," and
names aren't excluded in this overarching message of
the worth and value of words. There is the belief that
what you name a child will shape and/or define who
they become—that they will live up to what you call

them. Although it may or may not have some credibility, this belief was very influential in the naming of our children. So every time someone asks us what our children's names are, I feel a sense of pride knowing that their names were carefully and lovingly considered and chosen.

In this Advent season, I often think of how Mary truly felt. She had to have grappled with the weight of such a responsibility—being the mother of the One for whom all the world had been waiting. There was one burden she didn't have to carry: naming him. Although it was typical for the naming of the children to be the duty of the mother, this time the baby that was to be born was named by His Father, not by Mary or Joseph.

Matthew 1:20-21 (KJV) says, "But while he thought on these things, behold, the angel of the Lord appeared unto him in a dream, saying, Joseph, thou son of David, fear not to take unto thee Mary thy wife: for that which is conceived in her is of the Holy Ghost. And she shall bring forth a son, and thou shalt call his name Jesus: for he shall save his people from their sins."

This name meant something special. This name wasn't just thought up on a whim or conjured from the imaginations of well-meaning family and friends. This name was different. The salvation of the world depended on it. Acts 4:12 (KJV) tells us, "Neither is there salvation in any other: For there is none other name under Heaven given among men, whereby we must be saved."

Can you imagine if Joseph and Mary had gotten that one thing wrong? I can't. Mary and Joseph's obedience in this matter was of the utmost importance. It literally was the difference between life and death.

While the naming of our children is not typically done in the fashion of Mary and Joseph, I still believe God wants to be a part of how and what we name our children. I have met many mothers who, like the Bible character Hannah, named their children based on God's response to a specific prayer or circumstance. There are also family names that are passed down through generations, representing years of tradition. What I know to be true is that every time I say the name "Jesus," something shifts in my spirit. There is power in the name of Jesus, and rightly so.

The next time you hear the question, "What's his/her name?" take a moment and think about the name above all names, Jesus, and what a profound impact His name truly has in your life.

Let's pray: I thank You God for Jesus, and the salvation in His name. I also thank You that You have named me also—beloved, precious, beautiful, forgiven, blessed, Your child. Help me never to forget how wonderful the name of Jesus is and to call upon His name as my Friend, Brother, and Savior. Thank You for knowing my name, too, Lord, and calling me Your own. In Jesus's name I pray. Amen.

Alexis A. Goring

Devotionals about Faith and Praise

Devotionals for the *Heart*

www.capturingtheidea.blogspot.com

Praise: An Untapped Power

By Nanci Rubin

"I will bless the Lord at all times, His praise shall
continually be in my mouth."
– Psalm 34:1 (KJV)

I wish we understood more about the power of praise.

Do you know someone in the Bible who praised their
way out of a bad situation?

I'm reminded of Paul and Silas locked and shackled
in a dark, dank prison cell for the crime of preaching
Jesus. Paul didn't complain about his situation or the
tribulations he'd endured preaching the Gospel.
Instead, he praised God despite his circumstances,
just like we are also advised to do. According to
Philippians 4:4 (KJV), we are to, "Rejoice in the
Lord always: and again I say, Rejoice."

Despite their depressing circumstances, Paul and
Silas began to praise and worship God. They knew
how to release the untapped power of praise, and the
prison doors opened!

One of the quickest ways to release God's blessings
in our lives is to give Him praise. He inhabits the
praises of His people. You might ask, "How can I

praise Him when all of these horrible things are happening?"

Anyone can praise God when everything is going well, but it takes faith to praise God in the hard places. It takes faith to praise Him when you're surrounded by impossibilities. We need to thank Him for the victory. Thank Him for who He is. Praise encourages faith. Hope rises, and you focus on His ability to succeed in your life, not on yours to fail. God is for you.

There was a season in my life when I felt all was lost. At nine months of age, my daughter was diagnosed with cystic fibrosis. The doctors told us she would probably never live to age two. Hearing those words produced a malignant fear that gripped me by my throat and chocked out my hope. After hearing that diagnosis and prognosis, I roamed the hospital campus, moving like a sleepwalker, numbed and afraid.

I wish I could confess to you that I stood in faith for her healing. Well, I didn't—at least not right away. I allowed fear to control my life for an entire year, marking off the days until she turned two and thinking that on her second birthday, she would be "taken" from me. I believed the lies from the enemy. Yes, when you're down, he'll kick you a little more.

I began to speak God's truth over my situation and,

finally, the enemy's efforts no longer had a negative effect. As I praised God, I learned I could draw a line in the sand. You can, too.

Her second birthday came and went. My prayer life began to change. I started thanking God continually for her. I took my eyes off our circumstances. Praise became a powerful tool that dispelled the fear I'd lived with for too long. My child's courage and strength kept me moving forward. I praised God for the privilege of being her mom. We didn't allow her sickness to kill our joy. Praise extended her life, too. She passed away a few months shy of her sixth birthday. She'd lived beyond anyone's expectations.

Victory is always assured when you stand in faith on God's Word. And when you praise Him before you actually see your victory, it's then that you're giving Him a sacrifice of praise. He'll be faithful to intervene in your affairs and give you the desires of your heart.

Praise Him and see your mountains move out of the way!

Let's pray: Father God, thank You for keeping Your promises in our lives. I appreciate the promise that You will never leave us nor forsake us. In Jesus's name I pray. Amen.

God in the Graffiti: A Puerto Rico Love Story

By Jessica Brodie

"Forasmuch as there is none like unto thee, O Lord;
thou art great, and thy name is great in might."
– Jeremiah 10:6 (KJV)

Take a walk down Calle Palmas to the ocean in Arecibo, Puerto Rico, just past Avenida Victor Rojas, and you'll find a wide, well-tended sidewalk that borders the city and the sea. It's a popular spot, with joggers squeezing in a workout and couples strolling hand-in-hand, each pausing here and there to look north at the powerful, crashing waves and the jagged, ancient volcanic rocks that comprise the coastline. Beyond the sidewalk, it's a vista of untamed, natural, God-created beauty, wild and tempestuous at once.

It is there that I walked one rainy afternoon during my recent mission trip in the nearby mountains, struck by the glory of our Creator and the way humanity has made its mark alongside.

And as I walk, I see one word written over and over on the concrete planters that intersperse narrow benches along the sidewalk.

Dios.

God.

In electric blue and crimson spray paint, someone has written His name amid all this splendor, proclaiming God for the world to see.

Arecibo, and all of Puerto Rico, was hit by a double-whammy of hurricanes in Fall 2017—first Hurricane Irma Sept. 6 and Sept. 7, then Hurricane Maria Sept. 20—that devastated the island.

When I visited the island, half a year after the storms, a full sixth of Puerto Rico's population was still without electricity. Many left their homes to move to the United States mainland because they simply couldn't survive on the island any longer. Others whose treatment depends on electricity, such as dialysis or insulin or oxygen, have died.

Was the "Dios" writer crying out to God for help and mercy after the storm?

Was he or she joyfully proclaiming the name of the One, the Alpha and Omega, the Creator of the Universe—a shout of adoration for all to see?

Was the writer simply acknowledging God's singular importance, honoring our greatest commandment to love and lift up the Lord with all our heart, mind, and soul?

Dios. God. Whatever language you choose to use, whether it comes from your lips or sings in your heart, His name can move mountains and bring comfort. It can stop the devil in his tracks and keep temptation at bay. It can beg and praise and question and surrender all at once, say a million things in a single utterance, even when our intent might be limited to one. (He's too big for just one, no?)

Psalm 96:2-4 (KJV) urges, "Sing unto the Lord, bless his name; shew forth his salvation from day to day. Declare his glory among the heathen, his wonders among all people. For the Lord is great, and greatly to be praised: he is to be feared above all gods."

The prophet Jeremiah declares, "Forasmuch as there is none like unto thee, O Lord; thou art great, and thy name is great in might." (Jeremiah 10:6, KJV).

Sometimes spreading the Gospel is sharing our testimony. Sometimes it's bringing someone to church. Sometimes it's loving people in His honor.

And sometimes, it's spray-painting His name on concrete planters on the northern coast of Puerto Rico to remind passersby that no matter what else the day, the week, or this temporary human life can bring, at the end it's all about God.

What better way to love Him than to acknowledge

that?

Let's pray: Father God, help us to cry out Your Holy Name in good times and bad, in weakness and in joy. Help us remember You are the answer to everything and the Creator of the universe. And help us know in our hearts that You love us dearly. In Jesus's name I pray. Amen.

Living by Faith

By Nanci Rubin

"Now faith is the substance of things hoped for, the
evidence of things not seen."
– Hebrews 11:1 (KJV)

I think we all struggle in areas of faith. How do we
get it? How much do we need? Will I stand in faith
during the hard times?

God's Word says in Romans 10:17 (KJV), "So then
faith cometh by hearing, and hearing by the Word of
God."

How much faith do we need to move the mountains
in our way? Jesus said in Matthew 17:20 (KJV),
"Because of your unbelief: verily, I say unto you, if
ye have faith as a grain of a mustard seed, ye shall
say unto this mountain, remove hence to yonder
place; and it shall remove; and nothing shall be
impossible unto you."

We all have a measure of faith. From my own
perspective, I have learned in order for me to have
faith in the hard times, I have to stay "built up"
before they come. I strive to stay in God's Word and
prayed up so when the crisis arrives I won't be
caught unprepared. We should always be ready for

the unexpected. God is faithful, and we can trust Him no matter what comes our way.

Another criterion for water-walking faith is not to live in sin. The Bible says in 1 John 1:7 (KJV), "But if we walk in the light, as He is in the light, we have fellowship one with another, and the blood of Jesus Christ His Son cleanseth us from all sin."

As long as you walk in what light you have, there is cleansing from all sin by the blood of Jesus Christ. However, if you persist in living in wrongdoing, then you are going to get into trouble sooner or later. God extends His grace to us so that when we confess our sins, He is just to forgive us (1 John 1:9).

The sin issue is a biggie. We all sin. I often feel like Paul by doing the things I shouldn't and not doing the things I should. The older I get, the more aware I am of my shortcomings, but when I confess my wrongdoing God is faithful and reminds me He's not done with me yet.

In the 1980s, my husband and I were preparing for a life-changing trip to Israel. Where we lived at the time, there were many home invasions going on. Being away for ten days caused some concern, but I trusted God to protect what belonged to us. We had no family in the area but a wonderful older couple who lived next door. My husband was expecting a package to arrive while we were away, so I asked our neighbor if they would look out for it. They were happy to do so. Our trip was the most amazing trip of our lifetime—and our return home brought us a total surprise and definitely renewed our faith in God's promises to us as believers.

I walked over to our neighbors' not only to pick up our mail and package, but to give them the gift we'd picked out for them. That's when my neighbor told me what a wonderful alarm system we had. She eagerly related how when she opened the storm door to pick up the delivered package, the alarm went off. I had a huge smile inside me because that was God's alarm system. I couldn't wait to tell her that we didn't have an alarm system. We had prayed God would protect our home and, bless His name, He did. That was a wonderful testimony and an opening to witness to our precious neighbor.

I can't tell you how many times God has done the miraculous in our lives. I remember reading somewhere that God is as faithful as we believe Him to be. I strive to walk by faith. There are many areas where my faith is weak, but I work through the trust issues. I can honestly say He will be there when you call on His name. We can trust Him.

I hope this is an encouragement for you today. Our world is so stressed, and there are so many hurting people, especially our youth. I can't urge you enough to trust God with your loved ones and family. He is as close as your next breath. Things might appear hopeless and a situation impossible, but I can honestly say He has not forgotten you.

Remember that you have a measure of faith, and you can build it up by believing you are who God says you are. If we stumble and fall and make a mess of everything, God's not going to be mad at you. He'll be mad about you. He loves you more than you can imagine.

Let's pray: Father, thank You for the gift of Jesus and the knowledge that whatsoever we ask in prayer, believing, we shall receive, according to Your word. In Jesus's name I pray. Amen.

Rainbow Messages

By Paula Moldenhauer

"I do set my bow in the cloud, and it shall be for a
token of a covenant between me and the earth."
– Genesis 9:13 (KJV)

My nine-year-old burst through the front door. "Did
you see? There are two rainbows outside!" Our
family rushed to the window. I trailed behind, caught
up in a glum mood.

"Hurry, Mom!" my seven-year-old pleaded. "You
gotta see this!"

I caught my breath as I joined them at the window.
The perfect rainbow arched right in front of our
home. Its colors were so rich it looked surreal, like
something from a children's Bible storybook instead
of honest-to-goodness reality.

A tug in my heart said God gave me the rainbow to
remind me of His promises.

Like the grumpy woman I was that day, I rejected the
happy thought, reasoning with the left side of my
brain that science has shown us how and why
rainbows were made. The rainbow was delighting
many families throughout our neighborhood. It

wasn't personal. It wasn't a reminder to hope in God. Instead of reveling in the wonder of the rainbow's beauty, placement, timing, and perfection, I recited the colors that made up the rainbow.

Even people who've never read the Genesis account of Noah know the rainbow is a symbol of hope and promise. Whether or not God painted that rainbow for me at that moment can be argued either way. That isn't the point. The point is the Holy Spirit wanted to whisper hope into my heart as I gazed upon the rainbow's wonder.

But that afternoon, I didn't want to feel hopeful. It would mean choosing faith over whining and, quite frankly, I felt like complaining.

I shut my heart and turned from the glorious rainbow. Oh, outwardly I tried not to dampen the enthusiasm of my children. I said the right things. Smiled an outside smile. But on the inside, I willfully closed my heart to the gentle reminder of the Holy Spirit that God's promises were worth holding onto.

What a waste! I should have rushed down my stairs and flung open the front door (and my heart)! I should have run onto the lawn, my arms spread wide, embracing the promises of the Creator! I should have twirled in the street beneath the brilliant arch and laughed in joyful acceptance of His loving encouragement!

How about you, my friend? Are there gentle whispers of hope that you turn from?

Let's pray: Father God, help me to embrace the moments of hope that You give so freely. In Jesus's name I pray. Amen.

The Scent of Grace

By Paula Moldenhauer

"For we are unto God a sweet savour of Christ, in
them that are saved, and in them that perish."
– 2 Corinthians 2:15 (KJV)

Any parent of multiple children between the ages of
eight and eighteen knows the drill. Even when you
limit their outside activities, there are days when you
wish you could clone yourself.

I still remember one of many weekends years ago
when our family of six endured three straight days of
nonstop running. Two of our boys played in a hockey
tournament, and our daughter competed in a
gymnastics meet. Though the events were scheduled
close together, they were in three different
locations—none of which were on our side of town.

At the end of the push, we came home hungry and
tired. After eating out between events, I didn't feel I
could pull the "let's just get a pizza" card. I dug
through the fridge, coming up with a big bowl of
pasta and some veggies. Since I don't have much
storage in my kitchen, I have a pantry of sorts in our
garage. I put the noodles into heat and rushed out the
back door and down our steps, in hopes I had a jar of
spaghetti sauce in the cabinet outside.

As I came down the stairs, I noticed a few blossoms on the rose bushes by the garage door. I wanted to enjoy them, but instead, I cringed at the weeds in their bed. Sighing, I continued my mad dash toward the door.

Suddenly, I screeched to a stop.

The fragrance of roses filled my senses.

I paused only a second, but in that moment I felt God. The perfume of the flowers took me out of my hurry mode long enough for me to experience beauty and tugged me toward the Divine.

I wish I could tell you I chose to stop and embrace the moment. Or that I at least breathed a prayer of thanksgiving. But I didn't. I rushed into the garage, grabbed the sauce, and flew back up the stairs.

Real life consumed me. Feed the kids, clear the table, assign chores, sort the laundry, meet that writing deadline.

Later, gazing at the computer screen, too depleted to write, my mind went back to the rosebush.

Too often, I treat God's grace like I treated the rose. I catch a whiff of its beauty and rush on, noticing all the little weeds of my life instead of embracing the wonder of amazing grace. A grace He pours over me and through me like sweet perfume.

I stared at the computer for a while, longing for that rosebush. Finally, I pushed my chair back, releasing myself from the next task on my to-do list. I needed to, literally, stop and smell a rose.

A light rain had fallen, and the air outside smelled damp instead of perfumed as I tramped down the back steps. I went to the blossom, stuck my nose right in the middle of that flower, and inhaled deeply.

The fragrance was Heavenly. I spent a couple of minutes pulling the unsightly weeds, pausing every little bit to sniff the rose.

You see where this is going.

It's a joy to pause and let the wonder and beauty of Christ soak into our souls. When we inhale deeply of the fragrance of His character, the busyness, the irritations—the weeds—of life are more manageable. We recognize the sweet fragrance of His grace surrounding us, living in us, and flowing from us.

Let's pray: Dear God, how I need Your grace. Every day. Every hour. Every minute. Teach me to breathe deeply, inhaling its perfume. Whether life is a blur or a saunter, it's better when I dwell in Your fragrance. In Jesus's name I pray. Amen.

I'm FLAWed

By Paula Moldenhauer

"In the body of his flesh through death, to present
you holy and unblameable and unreproveable in his
sight."
– Colossians 1:22 (KJV)

It's hard to get through a day without noticing a flaw
in my appearance, in my behavior, or in my work. It
used to get me really down, because I am a
recovering perfectionist. Maybe you've conquered
this completely. But I haven't.

Most of us struggle with what to do when we see our
flaws or the flaws of someone else.

Recently, during a prayer time with some dear
friends, God showed us His perspective on flaws. He
reminded us that His blood has cleansed every
imperfection, and we stand before Him as blameless.
When He looks at us, He sees the person He created
us to be. He sees the new creation we are in Him. It's
like 2 Corinthians 5:17 (KJV) says, "Therefore if any
man be in Christ, he is a new creature: old things are
passed away; behold, all things are become new."

God sees a precious work of His very own hands, a
work He knit together in our mother's womb. If you

don't believe that, hang out for a while in Psalm 139.

Sure, God knows we struggle with faults. The psalmist says God knows we are, as it says in Psalm 103:14 (KJV), "we are dust."

But He isn't wringing His hands in despair when He sees our flaws. He already executed His perfect plan. He saved us, made us blameless in His sight, and is determined to change us from the inside out. He who started a good work in us will be faithful to complete it (Philippians 1:6). He works all things for our good to make us more and more like Jesus (Romans 8:28-29).

God is creative. He wanted to drive the point home, so during our prayer time, He gave my friends and me an acronym for FLAW:

Free to

Live

As

Worthy

I've had quite a journey learning to accept my flawed self. But if God is not worried about our imperfections, why are we? Our flaws don't have to bring shame and self-judgment. They don't have to lead to ugly, unhealthy thinking about ourselves.

How about a paradigm change?

The next time you are overcome with one of your flaws, try God's way of thinking. Even with that imperfection, remember: You are Free to Live As Worthy!

Stop and praise God for the work of the cross, the blood that changed you and made you righteous, redeemed, and holy. Thank Him for creating you and praise Him that everything He creates is good.

Accept yourself without pretending the flaw isn't there or judging yourself for its existence. Stand up straight in your identity as a worthy, blameless, beloved child of God. Turn your focus to praise for the change God is doing within you as He remakes you to be more like Jesus.

Then—from a mindset of one who is Free to Live As Worthy (even with a flaw or two, or two hundred)— ask Him to empower you to overcome.

Let's pray: Dear God, the next time that I recognize a flaw in myself or others, remind me that because of Your blood, we are Free to Live As Worthy. Instead of judgment, help me receive Your grace, mercy, and unconditional love. Then help me extend the grace You've given me. In Jesus's name I pray. Amen.

Alexis A. Goring

Gratitude Cultivates Joy

By Paula Moldenhauer

"Giving thanks always for all things unto God and
the Father in the name of our Lord Jesus Christ."
– Ephesians 5:20 (KJV)

Grandpa and Grandma's little brown house in the
country boasted a big front porch and a big heart. On
Thanksgiving, there wasn't room for everyone at the
table. This was not a fine china and crystal affair. Our
extended family would spill all over the house and
yard, our ample feast filling sturdy paper plates held
on knees.

Grandma baked for days. Pies were her specialty. She
also made homemade rolls, cornbread, and biscuits.
She served at least three kinds of potatoes so
everyone got his or her favorite—mashed, fried,
stewed. The aunts and cousins brought more food.
We never ran out of turkey. The family respected my
dad's status as preacher, and usually he gave the
blessing.

Grandpa and my uncles were storytellers, and I loved
to listen to them spin their tales of the old days. Our
family had its issues, but this was family at its best.
Good food and plenty of it, lots of teasing and
laughter, and extra hands to wash the dishes at the

end of the day.

It's good to take a day to focus on being thankful, but daily gratitude is more powerful than most of us understand. In Ann Voskamp's book *One Thousand Gifts*, she encourages people to journal notes of gratitude every day for a year. If you write three things a day, you'll have a thousand!

When I read that book, I had a hallway in desperate need of paint and a heart in desperate need of gratitude. It took me a year and a half to get to one thousand. I didn't write on my wall every day, but when I did, I dated the entry and wrote in brightly colored Sharpies until my mood lifted. I wrote of big things and small, like the fragrance of baking bread, my son's home run, and the joy of my daughter's marriage. When I studied that wall, it never ceased to amaze me how much good there is in this life. We don't notice the half of it.

A friend going through a hard time said God told her to, "Cultivate a capacity for joy."

I love that. He didn't tell her to get over the grief, just to make space for joy. Focusing on God's good gifts and thanking Him helps me cultivate a capacity for joy.

I no longer have a gratitude wall. (We won't talk about how many coats of paint it took to cover that sharpie list!) But I seek to write notes of gratitude on my heart and His. I pause and notice the gifts in each day and to make time for good things. Sometimes it's as simple as grabbing my cell phone and taking a picture of the sunrise or lighting a fragrant candle.

I'm not a huge football fan, but I thank God for the Broncos! The community my family has fostered around those "stupid" games (doesn't football last forever?) blesses me. There aren't too many things more joyful than the deep-throated roar of celebration that explodes in my basement when the Broncos score.

Autumn is the time of year I can buy my favorite apples. The fragrance of someone's fireplace often fills the evening air. I love sunsets and long walks, and even old bananas make banana bread.

Sweet friend, do you see it? The good all around us?

I challenge you to cultivate a capacity for joy. Notice your good God and His good gifts. Maybe it would help to write out things you're grateful for. Put them in a jar on the kitchen table and read them aloud to yourself. Write notes of gratitude in your journal. Maybe, like me, you need to do it even bigger, and so you write the thank you list in big, bright letters with red and purple and yellow Sharpies.

Let's pray: I give thanks to You, God, for You are

good and every good gift comes from Your hand. Help me cultivate a capacity for joy, noticing the beauty around me and embracing the good moments of life. In Jesus's name I pray. Amen.

Alexis A. Goring

Devotionals about Sharing your Faith

www.capturingtheidea.blogspot.com

A Labor of Love

By Jessica Brodie

"And whatsoever ye do, do it heartily, as to the Lord, and not unto men; Knowing that of the Lord ye shall receive the reward of the inheritance: for ye serve the Lord Christ."– Colossians 3:23-24 (KJV)

She had two-inch burgundy nails, glitter on her eyes, and the biggest smile I'd ever seen—and she made my day. Ringing up my purchases at the local megastore, this cashier chatted joyfully as she slid items across the scanner and into the bags. She smiled like she meant it.

I'd never met her before, but her attitude lifted my heart and made me want to know her. She represented the store well, and I'd be willing to bet she also represented her faith well. For she clearly was a Christian, and the words "Jesus" or "church" didn't even need to come out of her mouth for me to know that.

But, of course, she's an anomaly. Most times I'm at that store, I get a cashier who rarely makes eye contact, let alone mutters a "have a nice day." I get it. Years of working day in and day out can take a toll on a person. We become lost in the work, lost in the shuffle of busy-ness. We forget about the big picture—why we are working—and get sucked into whatever it is we are working on. Our perspective about life starts to change with this.

Defeated by the prospect of endless working, some people just seem to give up. They show up at their job, do just enough to get by so they don't get fired, collect their paycheck, and go home.

As Christians, that's not the kind of workers we are called to be. The apostle Paul had some important words about the work we do on earth. He wrote several times about the importance of working hard and giving our all. After all, the way we live our lives reflects our Lord. If we claim to be Christians but spend our time being lazy, mean-spirited, or selfish, we aren't reflecting our Lord in a good and proper manner.

In his letter to the early Christians in Colossae, Paul urged obedience and an upright, faithful life. He urged husbands and wives to respect each other, and the same for children and parents. And when it comes to work, he urged, "And whatsoever ye do, do it heartily, as to the Lord, and not unto men; Knowing that of the Lord ye shall receive the reward of the inheritance: for ye serve the Lord Christ." (Colossians 3:23-24, KJV)

Work is a given. We spend our lives at work, and while the pay varies, everyone has a job. Some work as parents, some as teachers, some as business owners, some as employees. Our challenge as Christians is to do that work as though we are doing it for Christ—for in reality, that's exactly Who we are doing it for. Everything about us—the way we live, the way we love, the way we speak, the way we think—comes back to the Lord.

We are to serve Him in all we do, at every moment. It's not just so we can represent our faith well, though that certainly is a bonus. But our work, all we do on earth, is tied up in our souls. When we greet a customer, we're greeting someone in the Lord. When we use our God-given gifts, whether that's working on a car or preaching the Gospel, it's all in the Lord. Nothing we do is too small or insignificant to matter. All we do is seen and noticed. And everything can point to Christ if we let it.

Think about how you can allow the work you do to glorify God and point the way to eternity. Is there anything you could be doing better to make that happen?

Let's pray: Lord, thank You for all the blessings You give us. Help us to do our work, whatever it is, as though we are doing it for You. Help us to have grateful and loving hearts that shine Your light to all. In Jesus's name I pray. Amen.

The Struggle is REAL

By Glynis Becker

"Fear thou not; for I am with thee: be not dismayed;
for I am thy God: I will strengthen thee; yea, I will
help thee; yea, I will uphold thee with the right hand
of my righteousness."
– Isaiah 41:10 (KJV)

A few years ago, a phrase became popular as a sort of punch line to funny pictures or ridiculous, first-world problems: "The struggle is real." You can laugh when it's attached to a picture of a puppy that can't quite make it up the stairs or a toddler in a high chair asleep with food on his face.

But the truth is, sometimes the struggles are very real, and sometimes they are not at all funny. At different points in our lives, each of us must deal with things we'd rather not. Some are a result of choices we've made. Sometimes they are simply circumstances of life in this world.

No one I know has ever asked for more struggles. I know I certainly never have. I think human nature is to make our lives as comfortable as possible. Just like water and electricity find the path of least resistance when flowing from point A to point B, we humans aren't much different.

People try all sorts of things to make their lives easier. Some manipulate others into doing their work for them. Some use alcohol or drugs to make their lives feel smoother, even if that really creates more problems in the long run. Some pour their hearts into things that don't really matter to avoid doing the more important, but harder, things.

God knows this. God created human nature, just like He created water and electricity. He knew how it would all turn out. Our laziness, our struggles, our dysfunction, and our choices are never a surprise to Him.

But what He does with those things can definitely surprise us. God can use the struggle of an addict to show His power, strength, and compassion. God can show the world His provision to one who can't make ends meet. God can show grace through someone and to someone struggling with a family relationship.

As believers, we need to be open in sharing our struggles with each other and with people seeking the faith. When others see how God steps into our hardships with us and carries us through, we have the most powerful testimony there is.

Our weakness and our difficulties prove to ourselves and others that God is near and that He cares about our lives. Often in those times, our faith becomes real. Why wouldn't we want more of that?

I'm certainly not saying I'm ready to pray for more difficulty in my life. But when the hardships come, and they will, I pray I see them less as a punishment and more as a journey to a new glimpse of God's power in my life.

Let's pray: Father God, help me to bear my struggles with confidence and peace, knowing that You are in them with me. Help me to be vulnerable with others, sharing my testimony of Your goodness to me through all the circumstances of my life. Show me how to help carry someone else's burdens, to encourage others, and to love the people You've placed in my path. Thank You for Your faithfulness, love, and care for me. In Jesus's name I pray. Amen.

The Comfort of Jesus

By Melissa Henderson

"Jesus Christ the same yesterday, and to day, and for ever."
– Hebrews 13:8 (KJV)

Have you ever paused to consider the Scripture listed above?

Have you ever thought about the blessing of Jesus staying the same yesterday and today and forever? What a wonderful comfort to know Jesus is always with us. He never leaves us. He loves us forever. In a world full of changes, the love of Jesus brings blessings to all.

Our days may be full of activities, rushing here and there, trying to complete everything on the to-do list. Or our days may be lonely and filled with uncertainty. Each of us has a unique path in life and special gifts given to us by God. Knowing He is with us brings comfort and peace.

As we experience daily schedules, sometimes things are the same and sometimes different. The schedule may include a different time or place. A new appointment, lunch date, play date, or our work hours may change. Births, deaths, illness and more. How we adapt to those changes shows others how we rely on God.

Even if our lives are filled with happiness or sadness, calm or stress, rest or rush, there is one constant in our lives: Jesus. Forever. Even if we become weary and lose hope, He never leaves us. We can always return to Him.

Friendships may come and go. New friendships may be formed. The hours change, the days change, and lives change daily. Change is evident everywhere, from the ocean tides to the rising and setting sun. Changes come in the seasons and with the weather. From warm temperatures to cold winds, God's creations are full of changes.

When we feel overwhelmed, Jesus is there, waiting for us to go to Him. When we are filled with joy and happiness, Jesus is there, waiting for us to go to Him. From prayers of anguish to prayers of thanksgiving, His attention to us never wavers. He never turns His back on us.

His arms are always open, waiting for us. His love is always evident. We are forever His.

Jesus is always the same. We never have to worry about losing His love or Him not caring for us.

Jesus loved us yesterday. Jesus loves us today. Jesus

loves us forever.

Can you share this good news with others? Have you showed His love to others today?

Find someone and remind them of Hebrews 13:8. Have a conversation about the peace Jesus provides.

There may be someone waiting to hear about the love of Jesus. Don't assume everyone knows the comfort of Jesus. Share His love through your words and actions.

What a glorious day to show people "Jesus is the same yesterday and today and forever."

Let's pray: Dear Jesus, I am very thankful You are the same yesterday, today, and forever. I am comforted in knowing Your love for me never ends. Help me show Your love to everyone I meet. In Jesus's name I pray. Amen.

Author Bios

Read on for the professional bios of each devotional author.

www.capturingtheidea.blogspot.com

Author Bio for Quantrilla Ard

Quantrilla (Quanny) Ard is a faith-based personal and spiritual development writer who lives in the Washington, D.C., metropolitan area with her husband and three littles.

In addition to being a dedicated wife and mother, she is an entrepreneur, doctoral student, and curator of all things lovely. As a woman on her own quest of shining a light on the shadowy, hidden places in her life, she writes as the "Ph.D. Mamma" about things she knows to be true in hopes to encourage others to do the same.

Her spiritual goals and her love for Jesus Christ propel her quest to share the journey with other women. She endeavors to walk alongside women and encourage them with words, deeds, and wisdom.

Quanny believes in the power in collective strength, community, and fellowship. You will find her wherever people are sharing stories of triumph.

Connect with Quantrilla via her website: https://www.thephdmamma.com.

Author Bio for Glynis Becker

Glynis Becker enjoys writing devotions, inspirational short fiction, novel-length fiction, and screenplays. Her film *Sinking Sand* is available for streaming at Amazon and TubiTv and on DVD.

She spent her childhood traveling the country as an Air Force brat until she decided to attend college at the South Dakota School of Mines and Technology. Once she got her mechanical engineering degree, she decided she couldn't leave, so she has made her home for the last thirty years in the beautiful Black Hills of South Dakota with her photographer husband, their two almost-grown children, and one very cat-like poodle.

She has worked as a software engineer for a defense contractor, an adult ministries director at a church, and currently does paperwork and intake for an adoption agency.

When she's not writing, working, or volunteering, you'll find her reading everything from Christian fiction to epic fantasy novels, watching TV, or cheering for her favorite sports team, the Minnesota Vikings.

Connect Glynis via her website: www.glynisbecker.com.

Author Bio for Jessica Brodie

Jessica Brodie is an award-winning Christian journalist, author, blogger, editor, and devotional writer.

She is the editor of the *South Carolina United Methodist Advocate,* the oldest newspaper in Methodism, which has won 113 journalism awards during her tenure.

Represented by Bob Hostetler of The Steve Laube Agency, Jessica is a seasoned speaker and contributor to Crosswalk, iBelieve, and the United Methodist News Service, among many others. She has a weekly faith blog at JessicaBrodie.com and is part of the team at Wholly Loved Ministries.

Her novel *Tangled Roots* won a third place Foundation Award in Contemporary Romance at the Blue Ridge Mountains Christian Writers Conference in 2019. An earlier unpublished novel, *The Memory Garden,* won the 2018 Genesis Award for Contemporary Fiction from American Christian Fiction Writers.

She is the author of *Feed My Sheep: A 40-Day Devotional to Develop a Heart for Hunger Ministry* (2019) and *More Like Jesus: A Devotional Journey* (2018) and editor of the anthology *Stories of Racial Awakening: Narratives on Changed Hearts and Lives of South Carolina United Methodists* (2018), all from her newspaper's Advocate Press.

Married, Brodie has four children and stepchildren and lives in South Carolina.

Connect with Jessica via her website: www.JessicaBrodie.com.

Alexis A. Goring

Author Bio for Sara L. Foust

Sara L. Foust is a multi-published, award-winning author and mother of five who writes surrounded by the beauty of East Tennessee.

She earned her bachelor's degree in animal science from the University of Tennessee, is pursuing her Master's in English through Southern New Hampshire University, and is a member of American Christian Fiction Writers. She is the author of the Love, Hope, and Faith Series, which includes *Callum's Compass* (2017), *Camp Hope* (2018), and *Rarity Mountain* (2019) and the Smoky Mountain Suspense Series.

Sara also has a story, "Leap of Faith," published in *Chicken Soup for the Soul: Step Outside Your Comfort Zone* and a novella titled *Of Walls*.

Sara finds inspiration in her faith, her family, and the beauty of nature. When she isn't writing, you can find her reading, camping, and spending time outdoors with her family.

Connect with Sara via her website:
www.saralfoust.com.

Author Bio for Melissa Henderson

Melissa Henderson is a writer of inspirational messages through fiction, nonfiction, devotions, blog posts, articles and more. Her first children's book, *Licky the Lizard,* released in 2018. She also has a story in the compilation *Heaven Sightings.* Her stories are included in other compilations, too.

Along with writing her personal blog and contributing to three other blogs monthly, her passions are sharing faith, enjoying time with family and friends, and volunteering in her church and community.

Melissa prays before writing and hopes the words she shares will bring the reader to a closer relationship with God.

Funny times in the Henderson family create great ideas for stories. The ability to laugh at everyday happenings can bring joy and blessings. The family motto is "It's Always A Story with The Hendersons."

Melissa is currently writing more inspirational messages, including young adult fiction, nonfiction, and children's stories.

Ideas come in each moment, and Melissa keeps a notepad close so these interesting thoughts can be ready to become the next story.

Connect with Melissa via her website:
http://www.melissaghenderson.com.

Author Bio for Gail Kittleson

An Iowa farm girl, Gail Kittleson appeared with her thick glasses and a pile of books at the local library counter every Saturday. Reading also facilitated her beginning understanding of God's love.

After graduating from Wartburg College and earning her master of arts in teaching English as a Second Language, she taught ESL and college expository writing. After publishing a memoir, the World War II bug bit Gail, and she's never been quite the same.

Her husband, Lance, has deployed with the Army several times. Between him and their son, she has experienced more deployments than anyone in the family. He shares her delight in historical research, their three grandchildren, and gardening in Northern Iowa.

Because it took so long for her to find her voice, memoir remains one of her favorite genres. She delights in helping other writers. Her workshops instruct and encourage authors on their journeys.

The Greatest Generation's tremendous sacrifices motivate Gail's fiction writing, and she desires to increase appreciation for veterans who ensured our freedom. She also does freelance editing.

Connect with Gail via her website:
http://www.gailkittleson.com/.

Author Bio for Paula Moldenhauer

Author, speaker, and mom of four, Paula Moldenhauer encourages others to live free to flourish. Though she met Jesus at seven years old, for many years Paula didn't understand the freedom she already had through his grace. In bondage to lies she believed about herself, God, and what she thought God expected, she got lost in intense self-hatred. But Jesus came to the rescue.

Paula is passionate about helping others find the glorious grace, truth, and new mindset that leads each of us out of what holds us back and into flourishing freedom.

She had been published more than 300 times in nonfiction markets and has a devotional book series,

Soul Scents. Her first published novella, *You're a Charmer Mr. Grinch,* was a finalist in the ACFW Carol Awards, and she now has six published works of fiction. Her most recent publication, *At Home with Daffodils,* is included in Barbour's *A Bouquet of Brides.*

Paula and her husband, Jerry, welcomed their first grandchild in May 2019. They treasure time with their growing family of adult children and their families.

Paula loves peppermint ice cream, going barefoot, and adventuring with friends.

Connect with Paula via her website:
www.paulamoldenhauer.com

Author Bio for Linda Wood Rondeau

Multi-published and award-winning author Linda Wood Rondeau is a veteran social worker whose books examine the complexities of human relationships.

Previously residing in Northern New York, the author now lives in Hagerstown, Maryland, with her best friend in life, who is her spouse of over forty years.

Though the author primarily writes fiction, her book, *I Prayed for Patience/God Gave Me Children,* is a critically acclaimed adventure in parenting. Her nonfiction book, *Who Put the Vinegar in the Salt/Called to a Higher Standard,* is scheduled to release in 2020.

Linda's most recent fiction work, *Hosea's Heart*, explores the complexities of the mandate to forgive as God has forgiven us. Her next fiction work, *Second Helpings*, is scheduled to release in 2020.

Her blog, Snark and Sensibility, hosts writers of various genres. In addition, she manages a Facebook page, Having the Prime of My Life, which provides a positive look at aging issues.

Connect with Linda via her website:
www.lindarondeau.com.

Author Bio for Nanci Rubin

Nanci hails from the lovers' state, Virginia, where she shares her life with her husband, Geoff, and their fur kids Roni, their Goldendoodle, and Romeo and Juliette, two semi-feral cats who have assimilated nicely into their home.

She is editing her debut novel, *The Longest Night*, a fiction inspirational historical romance with medical overtures. Nanci is a retired nurse and likes to inject a dose of medical procedures in her stories wherever she can.

Nanci belongs to Jerry Jenkins Writers Guild and is currently taking his novel-writing class. She has completed classes with Gotham Writers Workshop along with the Institute of Children's Literature. She belongs to the RWA and ACFW.

Her poetry has been published in *Free Verse, Commonwealth of Poetry* and the Poetry Super Highway. Some of her short stories have been published in *Whatever Lovely*. Her short story, "Lavender Gloves," won second prize in the Northern District Woman's Club of Virginia last spring.

Nanci is active in her church and is taking Rhema Bible College's Correspondence Course. She is also active in her local Woman's Club of Fredericksburg, a service-oriented club benefitting her local community. When not writing or studying she loves to garden, knit, read, and spend time with her husband, who recently retired.

Connect with Nanci via her website:
www.nancirubin.com.

Alexis A. Goring

www.ingramcontent.com/pod-product-compliance
Lightning Source LLC
Chambersburg PA
CBHW051944090426
42741CB00008B/1265